T0305822

Economics of
the Middle East
Development Challenges

World Scientific Lecture Notes in Economics

ISSN: 2382-6118

Series Editor: Ariel Dinar *(University of California, Riverside, USA)*

Vol. 1:   Financial Derivatives: Futures, Forwards, Swaps, Options, Corporate
Securities, and Credit Default Swaps
by George M. Constantinides

Vol. 2:   Economics of the Middle East: Development Challenges
by Julia C. Devlin

Forthcoming:
Lecture Notes on Econometric Models for Industrial Organization
by Matthew Shum

Cooperature Game Theory
by Adam Brandenburger

Lectures in Neuroeconomics
edited by Paul Glimcher and Hilke Plassmann

Economics of the Middle East
Development Challenges

Julia C Devlin
Brookings Institution, USA

W♭ World Scientific

EW JERSEY · LONDON · SINGAPORE · BEIJING · SHANGHAI · HONG KONG · TAIPEI · CHENNAI · TOKYO

Published by

World Scientific Publishing Co. Pte. Ltd.

5 Toh Tuck Link, Singapore 596224

USA office: 27 Warren Street, Suite 401-402, Hackensack, NJ 07601

UK office: 57 Shelton Street, Covent Garden, London WC2H 9HE

Library of Congress Cataloging-in-Publication Data
Devlin, Julia, 1966–
　Economics of the Middle East : development challenges / Julia C Devlin (Brookings Institution, USA).
　　pages cm. -- (World scientific lecture notes in economics ; v. 2)
　　ISBN 978-9814675185 (hc : alk. paper) -- ISBN 978-9814675192 (pbk : alk. paper)
　　1. Economic development--Middle East. 2. Economic development--Africa, North.
3. Middle East--Economic conditions--1945–　4. Africa, North--Economic conditions.
5. Middle East--Economic policy. 6. Africa, North--Economic policy. I. Title.
　　HC415.15.D486 2015
　　330.956--dc23
　　　　　　　　　　　　　　　　　　　　　　　　　　　　　　2015020387

British Library Cataloguing-in-Publication Data
A catalogue record for this book is available from the British Library.

Desk Editors: Chandrima Maitra/Philly Lim

Typeset by Stallion Press
Email: enquiries@stallionpress.com

Printed in Singapore

Contents

About the Author

Julia Devlin is a Lecturer in Economics at the University of Virginia where she teaches a course on the economies of the Middle East and North Africa. From 2012 to 2015, she was a Nonresident Senior Fellow at the Center for Global Economy and Development at the Brookings Institution in Washington DC and a consultant for the World Bank, among others. From 1999 to 2011, Julia was a World Bank staff member and worked on issues of trade and economic growth, private sector development and commodity dependence in the Middle East and North Africa region. She has published articles and books on these issues and has taught courses on economic development and the Middle East at Harvard University, the School of Advanced International Studies at Johns Hopkins University, the School of Foreign Service at Georgetown University and New York University. She has a Ph.D. in Economics from George Mason University (1995), an M.A. in Economics from the University of Virginia (1993), an M.A. in Arab Studies from the Georgetown University School of Foreign Service (1990) and a B.A. in Economics from the University of Virginia (1988).

Chapter 1

Growth in the MENA Region

Similar to other developing regions, Middle East and North Africa (MENA) economies achieved very high growth during the 1950s and 1960s with per capita GDP rising more than seven times from 1960 to the mid-1980s.[1] By the late 1970s and 1980s however, growth had collapsed and economic activity in many economies languished for nearly two decades. In the early to mid-2000s, growth accelerated rapidly, linked in part with higher oil prices and more favorable global economic circumstances.

For most countries in the region, growth performance is highly volatile. Turkey for example exhibits one of the most volatile growth patterns among middle income countries globally. The standard deviation of output or domestic demand growth in Turkey has been about twice the average in the G20.

The blueprint for this growth model emerged in the post-colonial period of the 1920s and 1930s and can be traced in a significant way to Mustafa Kemal Ataturk's policies of etatism, nationalism, modernization, and import substitution. Elements of this approach were adopted in greater and lesser degrees by many MENA states.

---

[1] The following discussion is based on Iqbal (2006), IMF (2013), Selected Issues, World Bank (2012), IMF (2013), Hansen (1991), World Bank (2000), World Bank (2003), Richards & Waterbury (1986), Beblawi (1987), Onis & Reidel (1999).

This chapter surveys growth performance in the MENA region with a focus on Turkey from the post-colonial period to the present. Section I discusses MENA growth performance and current challenges of growth facing the region, Sec. II surveys the emergence of the MENA growth model and Sec. III concludes with a discussion of factors contributing to the persistence of this growth model.

I. MENA Growth Performance

- Growth performance in the MENA region exhibits three main growth periods: high growth during the 1960s and 1970s, stagnation for much of the 1980s and 1990s, and a growth resurgence in the 2000s.

  o Over the 1960s, growth in real per capita GDP averaged 4.3%, the fastest rate among developing regions with the exception of East Asia and the Pacific.

  o During the 1970s, growth (real per capita GDP) slowed somewhat to 2.8%, although still outpaced most developing regions and the world average. However, by the 1980s, real per capita GDP growth was averaging less than 1% (0.5%) and 1.7% in the 1990s.

  o Since the 2000s, the region has witnessed a growth resurgence, with real GDP growth per capita averaging 2.6% outpacing all other regions with the exception of East Asia and the Pacific.[2]

- Today countries in the MENA region are predominantly middle and upper middle income countries.

  o Turkey in particular is an upper-middle income country with a population of 75 million and the 16th largest economy in

---

[2] Averages are based on WDI Annual percentage growth rate of GDP per capita in constant local currency. Countries selected are based on data availability for the period 1960–2009 and include Algeria, Egypt, Iran, Israel, Kuwait, Morocco, Oman, Syria, Tunisia, and Turkey. Data for 1960 averages cover the period 1961–1969, 1970–1979, 1980–1989, 1990, and 2000–2009.

the world. It is an EU accession candidate country, its largest trade partner, a member of the Organization for Economic Cooperation and Development (OECD) and the G20 and has ambitions to become one of the world's 10th largest economies in 2023 — the 100th anniversary of the founding of the Turkish Republic.

- Over the last 40 years, countries in the MENA region have made considerable gains and progress continues through the 2000s.

  o From the 1960s to the early 1980s, for example, rates of poverty reduction were among the highest in the world.
  o Today, most countries have virtually eradicated extreme poverty.
  o During the 2000s, per capita income in Turkey almost tripled and now exceeds US$10,000; poverty decreased from 28.1% in 2003 to 17.1% in 2008. Extreme poverty has virtually disappeared.
  o Turkey also made dramatic gains in health and education outcomes, maternal mortality rates declined from 29 deaths per 100,000 live births in 2005 to 16.4 in 2010 along with the rising access to education for girls. Primary enrollment is universal and secondary school employment is 69%.

- However, MENA economies have also developed economies exhibiting structural imbalances and vulnerabilities.

  o MENA countries in general are characterized by high rates of volatility in growth performance.

    ▪ Turkey has some of the highest growth volatility among large countries and globally with a standard deviation of output or domestic demand about twice the average in the G20. Every 10 years or so the economy finds itself in an economic crisis which has to do with a number of policy and structural features.
  o Domestic demand is a key driver of growth and external imbalances.

- The correlation between government spending and GDP, for example, is estimated at 0.61, significantly higher than in other emerging economies (0.06) and advanced economies (−0.53).

o Turkey is also characterized by structural current account deficits and an overvalued exchange rate.

- These current account deficits are linked with low levels of savings (as opposed to high investments) and a chronic excess of imports over exports. With higher domestic demand over the 2000s, for example, the Real Effective Exchange Rate (REER) increased by nearly 30% and the current account deficit grew from 0.3% to nearly 6% of GDP.

- The economy also has a structural bias towards imports and low exports. Since 2002, for example, goods exports have only grown by 3% points of GDP, while good imports have grown by as much as 9% points of GDP.

— Export shares of GDP remain small relative to comparator countries and the economy is relatively more closed. This creates a structural imbalance in Turkey's export structure relative to its buying (import needs).

— While Turkey's export volume has increased, its export prices have not kept pace with competitors in Poland, Brazil, and others. About one-third of the country's export income comes from primary sector-based and low-technology products.

- Turkey has also had limited success in attracting Foreign Direct Investment (FDI).

— While it has a large and growing domestic market and gateway to Europe (member of European Union (EU) Customs Union since 1995) Asia and the Middle East, FDI flows have been less than 2% of GDP over the 2000s and largely concentrated in non-tradable sectors (finance, telecoms, electricity) creating limited opportunities for export expansion.

II. What is the Source of MENA's Government-Driven, Inward-Looking Model of Growth?

- The blueprint for Turkey's growth model emerged during the 1930s under Mustafa Kemal later named Ataturk. The country became an early pioneer in using Import Substitution Industrialization (ISI) and economic planning and was of the first countries globally to experiment with a state-centric approach to growth which proliferated through much of the developing world from the 1930s to the 1960s.

- Turkey's early development strategy was part of a comprehensive transformation of state and society subject to the external constraints of the Lausanne Treaty and the legacy of the Ottoman Empire.

  o Ataturk and the Kemalists were born out of the Turkish Independence movement and represented a Westernized elite of military and civilian bureaucrats and intellectuals of the Ottoman empire.

    ▪ Strongly influenced by the ideas of 18th century Enlightenment and the rationalist, libertarian, and egalitarian philosophies of the French Revolution, Ataturk and the Kemalists outlined key priorities in terms of modernization, economic recovery, and development within the constraints of the Lausanne Treaty and the legacy of the Ottoman Empire.

  o Important external constraints on development included the Lausanne Treaty which stipulated the elimination of quantitative restrictions on foreign trade and freezing Turkish tariffs at prewar levels of 11%.

    ▪ At the same time, concessions were granted to foreigners which included the rights to impose taxes and collect tariffs.

  o There were limited indigenous industries or private investments. Under the Ottoman Empire, infrastructure investments had focused primarily on railways which were foreign-owned as were most banks and manufacturing; most indigenous industries were small-scale handicrafts which had suffered from low tariffs and import penetration.

- During the 1920s, Turkey's development was based on a relatively free trade and finance policy, subsidizing an inward looking infant industry program and promoting export-oriented agriculture.

  o It sought to create structural change in the economy and the building up of a modern industrial sector through support for private domestic and foreign investors and creation of state economic enterprises.

  o Private investors benefited from incentives and subsidies to new firms as well as state monopolies on sugar, tobacco, oil, and others — monopoly rights which were not exercised by the government directly, but were held by domestic or foreign firms under favorable terms.

    ▪ The government provided subsidies to domestic private firms under the Law for the Encouragement of Industry passed in 1927.

  o Support for agriculture attempted to improve the standard of living and boost the role of agriculture in the industrialization process through supply of raw materials and others.

    ▪ Policies focused on subsidies in input markets, such as, purchase of tractors and development of transportation networks to boost exports.

  o Ataturk did not discourage investment by foreigners and nearly one-third of firms created in the 1920s were joint ventures with Turkish and foreign investors.

- The shift to etatism occurred after 1929. Turkey was a primary commodity exporter and in many respects, Ataturk's statist approach was a reaction to the commodity price collapse and the Great Depression.

o Turkey's terms of trade fell by 23% in 1929 and another 33% in 1929–1934. To prevent a large trade deficit, Turkey implemented import controls through a wide range of measures, facilitated by the expiration of the Lausanne Treaty.

- Imports fell by 60% from 1929 to 1933.

o Imports were restricted through adoption of the first quota lists in 1931, eliminating imports of processed food, alcoholic beverages, clothing, shoes, leather goods, and others.

- However, imports of intermediate goods such as agricultural and industrial machinery, raw materials, and medicines were largely freely imported to support infant industries. Import licenses were distributed administratively and quotas provided huge rents to a limited number of exporters and producers.

o Disappointment with private industry also drove the strategy. By the 1930s Ataturk and the Kemalists' believed that private industry remained primitive and focused on appropriating rents created by import restriction and protection of the domestic market. Private firms were considered incapable or unwilling to build large scale modern industry.

- These sentiments were heightened by popular discontent in the aftermath of Great Depression and its impact on agriculture as well as charges of profiteering and corruption among private industrialists.
- With the introduction of etatism in 1931, the economy underwent a significant shift towards much greater state involvement in economic affairs for the purpose of accelerating economic growth.

o Basic features of etatism included:

- Widespread government intervention in the economy at large and balance of payment controls including price interventions (including trade), quantitative restrictions on trade and high levels of public investment in select sectors, primarily industry.

— Government control over domestic markets occurred through direct or indirect price supports for agricultural commodities and price controls for industrial goods along with wages in supported industries.
— Interest rates in financial transactions and banking activities were fixed by central authorities.
— The key distinguishing characteristic of etatism was the emergence of the state as a major producer and investor.

o State monopolies administered by private firms were transferred back to the public sector and foreign-owned maritime transport companies and railroads which had been nationalized in the Ottoman period were turned into state monopolies.
o The state also took on a direct role in large scale investment projects and as a producer of large scale industry and mining with the help of state-owned enterprises (SOEs) which became key actors in the development process.

▪ Development planning was based on five year industrial plans including a list of public investment projects in industry, mining, and energy. Many were financed with help from the Soviet Union and the UK.

• The etatist model delivered on growth but not employment.

o From 1932 to 1938, for example, GDP growth was over 7% and public investment more than doubled with high concentration in industry, education, health, and agriculture.

▪ Shares of manufacturing in GDP nearly doubled, rising from about 8% of GDP in the late 1920s to 13% by the late 1940s.

o However, the structure of industry did not change fundamentally.

- Employment remained concentrated in small scale and family firms which accounted for nearly 80% of employment in manufacturing and employment grew very little in large scale enterprises.
- Large scale, labor intensive private industries had been replaced by capital intensive large scale public industries heavily dependent on government financing.

o Agriculture expanded, growing by more than 6% over the same period although driven mainly by large increases in cultivated area.

- Unlike the case of Egypt, there was no redistribution of land through land reform, although the government distributed public, uncultivated land through grants to landless laborers and refugees amounting to about 6% of land cultivated around 1936, mostly in small lots. Overall such grants may have increased total cultivated area by about 20%.
- A shift towards industrial cash crops such as cotton and tobacco occurred although yields remained low due to growth in cultivation of less fertile lands and rising population pressure. Direct public investment was modest accounting for about 6% of total investment.
- Subsidized agricultural credit was provided through the Agricultural Bank in addition to agricultural price supports from the newly created Central Office of Soil Products established in 1932.

  — An increase in wheat tariffs provided protection along with wheat price supports through purchases conducted by the Office of Soil Products. Industrial crop prices such as cotton and tobacco were also supported through purchases made by state enterprises.

- Overall, however the distribution of income shifted away from agriculture towards non-agricultural sectors relative to the earlier period and large landowners producing for domestic and export markets suffered the largest losses with peasants and small subsistence farmers seeing higher income gains.

- By World War II, the etatist model was under increasing pressure.

  o World War II contributed to a decline of GDP by 37% together with diversion of resources for military efforts and policies such as forced delivery of agricultural products at low prices.

  o Growing domestic pressures and a new international order created the impetus for change.

  - There was a rising social unrest in the aftermath of the war effort and against a single-party regime (Republican People's Party). A new Democrat party was founded representing the interests of landowners, financiers, and merchants and led by former members of the RPP who gained widespread popular support.

  - Underutilization of agriculture was a primary rallying point.

  - Powerful urban interests also wanted to replace etatism with policies which better supported private entrepreneurship.

  - A development policy shift emerged which emphasized liberalization and agriculture.

    — This was supported by aid from the Marshall Plan and North Atlantic Treaty Organization (NATO) for reconstruction, development, and military purposes together with greater influence by the OECD.

- Thus, internal and external pressures pushed the Kemalist government (back) towards policies of private initiative and agriculture, playing down etatism and public industry and leading to a new interpretation of etatism which preserved a large role for the public sector in utilities, mining, and heavy industry, but promoted a transfer of all other public enterprises to the private sector.

- Free elections held in 1950 led to a victory of the Democrat party although with few tangible shifts in policy and economic structure; ultimately the economy became more entrenched in ISI.

  o Tariff structures created by Kemalists remained with the exception of liberalization of consumer goods imports which benefited from large terms of trade improvements after 1947 (due to the Korean War).
  o Low interest rates and lending to SOEs continued.
  o Investment did not shift towards the private sector.

     ▪ Public industry continued to dominate, rising from 25% to 35% of public investment.

  o Agriculture benefited more from improving terms of trade during the 1950s than explicit policy efforts.

     ▪ Terms of trade were generally 10% higher than in previous decades together with more favorable weather conditions.
     ▪ Mechanization of agriculture increased, supported in part by financing from the Marshall Plan — the number of tractors increased from about 1,000 in 1946 to 17,000 in 1950 and 42,000 at the end of the 1950s.
     ▪ Agricultural price support strategies which helped drive inflation however were expanded.

        — Support purchases were financed by the Agricultural Bank directly and indirectly through the Central Bank.
        — Agriculture expanded through mechanization and expansion of land under cultivation until the foreign exchange crisis (see in the following paragraph) which necessitated tighter import licensing and halted growth in tractors and crop area in 1956. Nevertheless, yields continued to stagnate during the 1950s.
        — One of achievements of the 1950s was improving distribution of income for the agricultural labor force.

  o Social insurance was introduced in 1946 and expanded through legislation during the 1950s.

- In Ottoman and Islamic societies generally, social security originated with the religious practices of the *zakat*, a charitable tax on net wealth levied on all believers.
- Added to this and under the Ottoman Empire, the first modern social security system was established as a military retirement fund set up in 1866 followed by a retirement fund for civil servants in 1881.

  — These were reorganized under the Kemalists and a Government Employee Retirement Fund was established by law in the 1950s. The social insurance system was further expanded during the 1960s but did not address unemployment.

- Labor legislation was also introduced requiring severance pay of 15 days for each year of employment after three years to be paid by the employer.

  — This system covered all people employed under service contracts except agriculture and the self-employed who were covered by a special organization established in 1970.
  — Employer contributions to the social insurance system were about 16–20% of the earnings with employee contributions about 12% resulting in a substantial insurance system and affecting the competitiveness of Turkish industry as well as income distribution. These likely had an effect on stimulating capital intensive technologies and contributed to unemployment.

- By 1953, foreign exchange reserves were nearly depleted due to the expansion of domestic demand and deteriorating terms of trade.

  o A decade of high domestic demand and inflation together with weak exports had contributed to the crisis.

    - Central bank financing of deficits of SOEs including agricultural price support contributed heavily to inflation.

- Nearly four-fifths of government claims on the banking sector were generated through credit extended to the private sector including residential construction and mechanization of agriculture.
  - o To deal with an impending foreign exchange crisis, import licensing was reintroduced, including for capital goods.
    - This helped create a vicious cycle based on price controls which tried to keep down the cost of living, higher agricultural support prices, rising SOE deficits to be financed through further credit expansion with increasing inflation.
    - Tightened licensing of exports and imports and import surcharges and export premiums also created a complex system of multiple exchange rates.
  - o The system came to an end in 1958 when foreign financing was no longer available and issuing of import licenses ended.
  - o Real exchange rate appreciation rose significantly from 1935 to the mid and late 1950s due to strong accelerating inflation relative to trade partners.
  - o Thus, the *de facto* import substitution policy of the Democrat party went way beyond the Kemalists of the 1930s.

- A full-fledged balance of payments (BOP) crisis and stabilization program began after 1958 followed by military rule in 1960–1961.
  - o A military takeover in 1960 was linked with suspicions that the Democrat government would not implement a full stabilization program.
  - o In 1961, to a new Constitution imposed comprehensive development planning with a mixed economy and inward looking import substitution policies together with liberalization of the labor market.
  - o The stabilization program included devaluation and unification of the Turkish Lira (TL) together with consolidation and

rescheduling of debt along with import liberalization, export regime changes, removal of price controls and increases in SOE prices.
o It also included reduced credit to the government and SOEs as well as the private sector.
▪ Growth in rates of money supply fell from 20% annually during the 1950s to 9% in 1959–1961.
o The economy was in recession for nearly four years as a result of the stabilization program and the balance of trade continued to deteriorate, undermining its objectives.
o Creation of the State Planning Organization in charge of proposing and implementing plans for economic, social, and cultural development was ratified by law in 1960 putting in place planning with medium five year plans and detailed annual plans.

- The period between 1962 and 1979, was characterized by relatively high growth and high unemployment, rising imbalances, parliamentary democracy, and military takeovers.

o Military sponsored governments from 1971 to 1973 did not change these basic policies although the second military takeover in 1980 endorsed private enterprise and a liberalization-oriented program with the help of international donors.
o Growth during the 1970s was higher, relative to the 1950s (Ataturk) and 1960s (Menderes Democrat Party) increasing from 4% to 6% and per capita growth from 2% to nearly 4% and above middle income averages (3.6%).
o Capital investment was the primary focus of planners with fixed gross investment increasing to about 22% of GDP from 15% during the 1950s.
▪ Total factor productivity (TFP) was estimated to have grown by 2% per year from 1963 to 1976. Productivity in agriculture however remained low at less than 1%.

o The first Five Year Plan began in 1963 and was heavily influenced by Jan Tinbergen, Chairman of the UN Development Committee.

- Growth targets of 7% were adopted and increased to 8% under the second Five Year Plan with Ataturk's etatist philosophy as the basis of the plan.
  - 50% of all investment was to be in the public sector guaranteeing a mixed economy.
  - Inflationary financing of public expenditures was not banned by the new Constitution and budgetary policy became the major policy instrument.
  - Investment was oriented towards import substitution with foreign exchange controls, import and export licensing, tariffs, and others.

o From the 1960s to the 1970s, large increases in the total budget (current plus capital) occurred, rising from 5% of Gross National Product (GNP) (1962–1963) to 12% in 1979–1980.

- This was linked with increases in public investment from 6.8% in 1962–1963 to 10.8% in 1979–1980. Private savings fluctuated during this period, rising and falling with worker remittances.

o Monetary expansion through the budget was also inflationary especially through the public sector after 1974.

o After the first oil price and lower worker remittances in 1973–1974, national borrowing rose sharply through the 1970s. Goods and services deficit continued to rise.

- Authorities were unable to simultaneously cope with both problems of rising fixed investment and higher oil prices.
- Losses in terms of trade were massive and amounted to nearly 5% of Gross National Income (GNI) (at factor cost).
- Lower remittances caused by immigration restrictions in Europe and by uncertainty about the future of the Lira

and the government's foreign exchange policies together with attempts to expand investment at a time when external balance of payment difficulties arose without being properly addressed led to a BOP crisis in 1978.

- Gross foreign assistance played a role for much of the 1960s and 1970s but diminished towards the late 1970s.

o Agriculture was no longer a leading sector for growth and became exclusively dependent on increased yields (real GDP per ha) through intensification of cultivation, improved plant varieties, and increased inputs of chemicals and tractors.

o Growth rates of manufacturing were virtually unchanged although manufacturing became the leading sector in terms of contributions to total growth.

- It did not compensate for the decline in agriculture.

o Unemployment increased from less than 2% of the labor force in the 1960s to 7% in 1977, linked with higher population growth, declining labor demand in Europe, rising foreign exchange difficulties and rising real wage costs particularly during the latter half of the 1970s.

- As agriculture shed employment, (72% of labor force to 54% from 1962 to 1977), industry shares increased modestly from 8% to 10%, migration by 4%, unemployment increased by 5%.

— Remaining workers were absorbed by construction and service sectors.

- Modest employment growth in industry was linked with rising capital intensity generated by high levels of capital investment, tariff, and exchange rate policies together with unionization and minimum wage legislation.

— Employment policies which forced public enterprises to employ more labor than needed likely led to inefficiencies and labor redundancies rather than adoption of labor intensive technology.

— In 1978, the government also committed itself to an incomes policy, although negotiations between the government and the Turkish Labor Confederation resulted in little restraint on wages.

o Foreign trade and export growth remained low, a characteristic of the Turkish economy since the founding of the Republic and linked with import substitution policies.

▪ One weakness of ISI strategies is that countries become more, not less dependent on imports and vulnerable to foreign exchange availability.
▪ The economy was also characterized by a strong anti-export bias.

— Steady exchange rate appreciation from 1948 to 1979 was interrupted by major devaluations in 1958–1960 and 1970.

⇒ Exchange rate adjustments occurred more frequently towards the latter half of the 1970s as the credit policy regarding the public sector became inflationary and development policy overambitious.
⇒ Discrimination against exports was endemic and created by multiple exchange rates, duties, taxes, and subsidies as well as licensing for imports and exports.
⇒ This bias was eliminated somewhat with tariff revisions undertaken to prepare for Turkey's membership in the European Union (EU).

• In 1980, the economy underwent a significant shift in policy with introduction of a reform program.

o A radical and surprise plan was adopted to stop the vicious cycle of hyperinflation, stagnation, and unmanageable balance of payment deficits.

- ■ It also ended etatist policies and included vast policy and institutional changes including:

  — Devaluation of the TL against the dollar by 33% and limitation of multiple exchange rate practices, greater liberalization of trade and payments regimes, export promotion, price increases for state traded goods and elimination of price controls, more competition for SOEs and elimination of government subsidies, higher interest rates, promotion of foreign investment, arrangements for consolidating private commercial debt and tax reform.

  — Income policies mainly constraints on union activities and collective agreements were also on the agenda.

- • After rising domestic political destabilization and accelerating terrorism, there was a military coup in September 1980 when Turgut Ozal came to power and endorsed the reform program.

  ○ Reforms were supported by structural adjustment and sectoral adjustment lending from the World Bank and International Monetary Fund (IMF) with total assistance including support from Saudi Arabia totaling US$4 billion.

  ○ With the military takeover in 1980 came a ban on militant unions and establishment of a Supreme Arbitration Board authorized to facilitate collective agreements and issue wage guidelines for future agreements.

    ■ Strikes were declared illegal. At the same time however, repressive measures were counterbalanced by restrictions on layoffs in manufacturing.

  ○ A new Constitution was adopted in 1982 followed by general but restricted elections in 1983 which gave Ozal an absolute majority.

    ■ In December 1983, the reform program was further refined to promote liberalization and market orientation and deal with social problems.

- However, in spite of these efforts, stabilization and liberalization proved to be a long drawn out process beginning in 1978.

  o Liberalization from 1978 to 1985 proceeded through exchange rate depreciations, wage constraint with relaxation of price controls, domestic financial decontrol, liberalization of trade, tax reform and some liberalization of capital movements.

    ▪ However, weaknesses of the program included the inability to control inflation and the budget deficit together with few socially oriented features of the liberalization program.
    ▪ Inflation reached 40% in 1985, approaching hyperinflation again in 1988. Monetary expansion driven by Central Bank financing of the budget deficit since 1975 was the primary culprit. The overall budget deficit after temporary improvements in the early 1980s remained high and partly hidden in extra budgetary funds.

  o State enterprises were required to adjust prices to reflect actual costs and basic subsidies remained on only a few commodities such as bread, sugar, coal, and fertilizers.
  o A market-oriented approach to agricultural support prices was adopted and implemented to make agricultural prices follow world prices.
  o In 1985, the role of the Wage Arbitration Board was curtailed and collective bargaining was liberalized although the ban on militant unions remained in force. By 1987, the Arbitration Board was abolished.
  o Institutional interest rates were raised considerably from 1979 to 1982 to offset negative real interest rates in 1980.
  o From 1974 to 1978 to 1983 there was a decline in private investment with no sign of increase in private savings.
  o Import restrictions were reduced as imports were transferred from highly restrictive to less restrictive lists and procedures simplified.

- ▪ After 1980, exporters were allowed to import inputs duty free and benefited from export incentives such as direct tax rebates for industrial goods.
- ▪ There were also significant reductions of tariff rates but mostly applied to capital and intermediate goods while consumer goods might have experienced tariff increases. So import substitution was not entirely abolished.

- o Tax reforms introduced from 1981 to 1985 helped to adjust tax brackets and marginal rates of taxation.

  - ▪ Taxes on agricultural income were also raised with the number of tax-exempt farmers reduced.
  - ▪ Corporate income taxes were unified in 1981 with rates adjusted upward and SOEs subjected to income tax.
  - ▪ A value added tax of 10% was introduced in 1985 to replace nine production taxes.

- o Foreign exchange restrictions related to capital movements were also replaced.

  - ▪ Residents and non-residents were allowed to hold foreign currency and open foreign exchange accounts with no restrictions on the use of these funds.

- • Between 1981 and 1985, per capita growth was about 2.4% less than two-thirds levels of 1961–1963 and less than half of levels in 1977–1979. Unemployment increased to about 12% by the mid-1980s.

  - o Thus, reforms were not able to reverse the employment trend and bring unemployment rates back to levels of early inward looking growth.
  - o External conditions had also become more difficult with labor migration to Europe halted and terms of trade moving against Turkey until 1984.

- • The most successful component of the reform was the increase in exports of goods and services which increased from 5% of GNP in 1975–1979 to nearly 20% in 1984.

○ Of this about 75% originated in manufacturing industry.

○ At the sector level, exports were facilitated by elimination of idle capacity in existing enterprises related to low levels of investment and slow growth which pushed more domestic production into exports.

○ There was also a shift in the composition of exports from agriculture-based exports which declined from 91% in 1962 to 36% in 1984 and a rise in semi-finished and finished manufactures from 1% to 46%.

▪ From 1978 to 1979 to 1982–1985, exports of industrial products increased by US$3,854 million.

▪ About 45% of the increase in exports was in consumer goods, mainly textiles and clothing, processed agricultural products and hides, or so-called light industries which were given low priority in the first four–five year plans. By 1985 and 1986 however, exports of iron and steel, metal products and machinery, chemicals, and others were also accelerating.

▪ Among the factors contributing to this boost was the Iran–Iraq War and higher demand from Organization of the Petroleum Exporting Countries (OPEC) producers and MENA countries, together with the impact of liberalization policies.

▪ Another important factor boosting export competitiveness was the strong decline in product wages after 1980, that is, real wages in terms of manufactured output (value added).

— High real wages had its origins in the Constitution of 1961 and early etatism of the 1930s. Real wage rates increased at a rate of 6.8% per year from 1965 to 1977 while labor productivity in terms of GDP increased at a rate of 4.7%.

— From 1977 to 1984, however, this development was radically reversed with productivity rising by 2.3% and real product wages falling by 10% annually. In

1984, real wages in manufacturing in terms of GDP
were basically back to levels of 1965.

- Overall, rates of increase in total factor productivity were only
  moderately higher however compared with earlier periods rising by 1.4% from 1973 to 1987.

  o Over shorter periods however there was an improvement
    from about 2% in 1973–1976 to 3.5% in 1985–1987. This was
    linked with increased capacity utilization and reduction in
    overstaffing as well as transfer of technology through liber-
    alized imports of capital goods.
  o Total public sector deficits still averaged 5% of GNP although
    the BOP improved with lower current account deficits.

- By 1986, public investment was expanding rapidly again rising
  to 16% of GDP in 1985 from an average of 2.5% per year from
  1982 to 1984. Higher than anticipated current account deficits
  had to be financed by short term borrowings and rose to about
  22% of total debt at the end of 1986.

  o Again the issue arose as to whether the Turkish economy
    could maintain such a high rate of growth without under-
    mining the stabilization and adjustment programs.
  o By the mid 1980s, the practice of transferring government
    resources to Special Budgetary Funds was loosening the
    effectiveness of expenditure controls.

- Average growth during the 1990s was below the 1980s at 3.9%
  relative to 5.3% and the economy remained vulnerable to persis-
  tent fiscal imbalances, chronically high inflation, and sharp
  business cycle fluctuations. Per capita income growth during
  the 1990s was about 2.1%.

  o This was a period of unstable coalition governments with
    frequent changes in ministers and senior officials.
  o A financial crisis in early 1994 coincided with public sector
    borrowing requirements of over 10% of GNP the previous
    three years.

o   Sharp adjustment followed a 1994–1995 stabilization pack-
    age and led to renewed discipline, but this was dissipated
    by sharp increases in public sector investment and generous
    increases in agricultural support prices and transfers to prop
    up weak state banks.

o   After a severe recession in 1994, the economy went through a
    boom period of the earlier-mentioned trend growth between
    1995 and 1997 linked with strong export performance stimu-
    lated by the real depreciation of the TL in 1994 and new mar-
    kets opening up in Commonwealth of Independent States
    (CIS) countries.

   ▪ Exports of goods and services grew by 16% per year
     between 1994 and 1997. There was also a strong boost to
     business confidence and investment from the 1996 customs
     union agreement with the EU.

   ▪ Access to external financing however was restrained and
     the government was forced to rely on monetization and
     deficit financing, leading to inflation and a rapid accumu-
     lation of domestic debt.

   ▪ By 1998, inflation was more than 100% and the govern-
     ment launched another stabilization program. With early
     elections in 1999, expansion was again triggered with
     public sector wages increasing from 7% to 8% of GNP.

   ▪ By late 1999, the public sector deficit had increased from
     4.6% to 13.6% of GNP and public sector debt rose from
     44.5% to 58% of GNP.

o   There was also little progress in structural reforms in bank-
    ing, energy, agricultural subsidies, and the pension system.

   ▪ State-managed pension schemes based on defined benefit
     financed on a pay-as-you-go basis were becoming the
     most urgent fiscal problem.

      — Problems included lack of a minimum retirement age,
        weak links between contributions and benefits, and
        others.

- State monopolies dominated energy and communications together with weak legal and regulatory frameworks.

  — In the power sector lucrative build operate transfer projects were awarded without open bidding.

  — Electricity tariffs for these contracts were set at more than double rates in other counties.

- In agriculture, price supports for select crops introduced during the 1930s had expanded in the 1960s and 1970s to cover 22 crops. Support prices were announced by government decree each year and related SOEs and agricultural sales cooperatives were committed to buy at announced floor prices. In addition, credit subsidies in the form of short term investment credit were subsidized by the government at interest rates well below inflation and commercial rates. Between 1994 and 1999, losses for SOEs in agriculture estimated at US$6.2 billion between 1994 and 1999. Support went primarily to larger and wealthier farms.

- The banking system remained burdened by chronically high inflation, large public sector borrowing requirements, and the use of tax breaks to favor placement of government debt over private sector borrowing.

- A new economic program founded on fiscal adjustment and deep structural reform was agreed in late 1999 but quickly followed by another boom-bust cycle and a full-fledged currency crisis.

  o It featured a pre-announced crawling exchange rate peg and matching fiscal deficit designed to reduce inflationary expectations and lower real interest rates.

  o However, rapid recovery of the economy in 2000 and low nominal interest rates led to a consumer boom and rapid import growth.

    - Consensus among coalition partners was hard to sustain during the boom and the government delayed on further fiscal tightening.

○ By 2001, the economy was in deep crisis.

■ Underlying factors were huge fiscal imbalances built up over the 1990s and accumulation of systemic banking sector risks.

■ An initial consumption boom was soon dissipated in the loss of confidence in the crawling peg exchange regime used as the main nominal anchor for disinflation.

■ Foreign creditors pulled back with a widening current account deficit and the government responded by taking over a major private bank and ending a blanket guarantee to bank creditors.

— This in turn raised concerns about fiscal sustainability and the problems culminated in a full-fledged currency crisis in 2001 which forced the government to float the TL and bail out the banking system.

• A crisis response program was launched in 2001 after collapse of the peg and devaluation with support from IFIs.

○ The largest ever support program from the IMF, in the amount of US$16 billion followed and the economy launched a new round of reforms.

■ Key components included restoring public financing through tightening of fiscal policy and public sector reforms and governance, renewed privatization and further liberalization in energy, telecoms and agriculture as well as extending social assistance to help low income groups affected by the crisis.

○ By 2002, the economy had recovered with GNP increasing by more than 7.8%, driven heavily by exports and tourism receipts.

■ Net public deficits had declined from over 90% of GNP in 2001 to 45% in 2006.

○ Growth remained high from 2002 to 2006 at 7.5% per year on average. Moreover, unlike previous decades, growth in the

2000s has been heavily driven by the private sector, private consumption, investment, and export growth.

o Inflation in 2004 had declined to single digits for the first time in more than 30 years.

- This was facilitated by a program of fiscal consolidation and in 2006 the Central Bank introduced inflation targeting.
- Primary fiscal surpluses were driven by higher tax revenues and better performance of SOEs with an overall deficit of about 2% of GNP.
- Net public debt fell to 64% in 2004 from 70% in 2003 along with lower real interest rates.
- Increasing capital inflows and growing interest in Turkish government paper allowed the Treasury to service the debt.

o Banking sector reform included establishing independence of the Central Bank as well as restructuring of the banking system.

o Agricultural price support subsidies were drastically reduced and replaced with direct income support.

o Privatization accelerated with FDI flows reaching nearly 20 billion in 2007.

- In 2005, Turk Telecom was privatized raising US$6.6 billion followed by the state refinery and the steel company.

o Social security reform was also instituted.

- Nevertheless, vulnerabilities remain. Higher growth was accompanied by a rising current account deficit due to rising imports of capital and intermediate goods as well as higher energy prices. Shares of long-term capital and non-debt creating flows have increased and provided financing for the current account.

o Despite the introduction of fiscal targets and expenditure ceilings with the help of a Medium-term Budget Framework in 2006, there are large deviations from expenditure ceilings namely personnel related expenses, current transfers which include transfers to social security, subnational government, and SOEs as well as goods and services.

- ■ Turkey's pension system is still very generous in terms of conditions for retirement (length of service required to be eligible is well below current OECD averages) and amounts — the ratio of average gross pension to average grow wage is very high.
- ■ Between 2005 and 2012, Turkey's civil service wage bill increased by 1.4% points of GDP growing from 23% to 28% of total expenditure. A collective bargaining mechanism introduced in 2012 has compounded the problem, with salaries negotiated in line with expected inflation. Employment has also increased by nearly 5%.

- In spite of considerable reforms over the 2000s, government as the driver of growth in Turkey also has its limits.

  - o IMF estimates assess that Turkey's average sustainable growth rates are about 4% (or the speed limit of growth is about 2–3% to maintain a stable current account) without incurring growing current account deficits.

- Thus, Turkey's development policies from the 1950s through the 2000s created rapid growth and industrial capacity but they also created a domestic market with heavy reliance on expansionary demand policies and external resource flows.

III. The Political Economy of Development in the MENA Region

- A remarkable feature of development policy in Turkey and the MENA region generally is the tendency for persistence.

  - o Over time, policy choices have contributed to strong but volatile growth performance and an economic structure highly vulnerable to global and domestic pressures.
  - o Economic structures have emerged and persisted and can be characterized as mixed economies with high shares of government involvement in terms of employment, production as well as regulation, weak global export performance, low levels of private investment (including FDI) and high unemployment.

- How can we explain the persistence of this MENA growth model across countries in the region and long periods of time?

  ○ One approach sees MENA states as highly interventionist, redistributionist states with high levels of social transfers according to an "implicit social contract" between governed and government.

    ▪ But this model may go too far in implying an almost Marxist redistribution of wealth and a tightly state controlled economy when the reality is more complex.
    ▪ Generally most countries are characterized by a large state and government apparatus functioning in a capitalist but mixed economy.

  ○ A related view emphasizes the role of "rentier" states or states which rely heavily on external rents (i.e., oil revenues, remittances) rather than domestic populations to generate growth.

    ▪ Some studies point out that this model may overstate the role of rents in shaping economic activity — most economic activity across a range of countries is based on rents and rent seeking to varying degrees.

- The view taken here is that both of these models apply to some extent, when approached from higher levels of generality.

  ○ Development policy choices and outcomes in the MENA region are in fact influenced by three key factors: external conditions, elite, interests, and institutional factors (see Figure 1).

    ▪ Most countries in the region are small, relatively open developing economies with the implication that external factors play a significant role in development performance.

      — In the case of Turkey, external factors related to the EU have had a clear impact on trade and external financing prospects and thus growth performance.

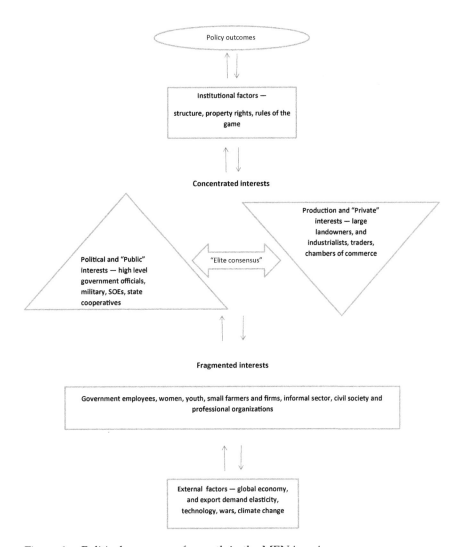

Figure 1.   Political economy of growth in the MENA region.
Source: Author. Adapted from Ekelund & Tollison (1997) and Devlin (2010).

— Thus, global economic conditions, wars, population growth, technology, climate are all factors considered "exogenous" or not under direct control by policy makers yet at any point in time exert critical influence on policy choices.

- Elite interests and consensus, primarily across public and private actors sectors play a role.

  — Political scientists frequently emphasize dynamics created by a gap between state autonomy and capacity in which a bureaucratic elite devises a notion of the national interest which is autonomous from any specific group and therefore must define and build a broader national coalition in order to implement this agenda and remain in power.

    ⇒ In this process, government officials play a key role in mediating and uniting coalitions of the corporate sector and upper level bureaucracy with broader national coalitions including small business, lower level bureaucracy, labor, and peasants.
    ⇒ Macroeconomic policy thus becomes endogenously determined by the government's growth and coalition building objectives.

  — A related perspective proposes that development choices are in fact the outcomes of elite-led "games" whereby elites represent ideological and political leaders and their clients.

    ⇒ Elites in this case are broadly defined groups such as ideological and political leaders and their clients (agriculturalists, industrialists, labor, civil servants) as well as day to day government functionaries, namely planners, bureaucrats and technocrats.

- Thus, the view taken here is that elite interests and consensus and more specifically the building of a national coalition and policy around an elite agenda is central to understanding development policymaking in the MENA region. Mid-level civil servants, youth and small enterprises as a group support this consensus at times and at other times oppose and challenge it.

— Development policy choices in MENA countries reflect a consensus, a "moving" equilibrium built on consensus arising from a relatively small number of people-namely ruling families/parties, large private industrialists, traders large farmers, military officers, and in some cases religious and ideological figures.

— Macroeconomic and economic reforms and strategies thus become endogenously determined, focused on maintaining an equilibrium of elite interests and creating a national consensus or popular support for this agenda.

- A historic account of agricultural reforms in the latter part of the 19th century sheds light on this dynamic, namely "...Whatever pressure there may have been to introduce a ... system of registration, taxation or private property rights, the actual result of policy was generally a bargain between the central government, local councils and men of rural power which was clearly neither in the interests of efficient administration nor the most profitable development of the region's agricultural resources" (Owen, 1981).

- Rent seeking naturally plays an important role in forging elite consensus particularly between bureaucratic and business elites.

  — In the early days of the Turkish Republic, for example, Ataturk adopted a system of import tariffs and financial incentives to encourage private business and industry.

  — Such incentives to private business and market restrictions confer high rents and create significant incentives for rent seeking behavior.

- However, rent seeking on a micro level does not do as well in explaining overall development approaches and large shifts in strategy such as Turkey's shift towards greater export orientation during the 1980s. The role of external factors and institutions or structures must also be considered.

— Once the basic strategy and institutions are in pace then rent seeking begins.

o   Institutional factors in particular constrain choices over time.

- Structures, rules of the game, property rights, and other institutional mechanisms influence policy choices and outcomes.
- Over longer periods of time, such rules and organizations make it difficult to undertake significant policy shifts.
- Policies of agricultural price supports and credit subsidies, for example, necessitate creation of state agricultural banks and purchasing entities, cooperatives which begin to exert their own pressures on the system while policies of industrialization and trade protectionism empower customs agencies and industrial SOEs.

   — Once created, such entities exert their own demands on the system and constrain policy choices.

- How do these three factors interact to affect policy choices?

   o   The confluence of all three factors can be seen in the significant shift of Turkey's development strategy during the early 1980s.

- Following nearly a decade of rising fiscal and current account deficits together with rampant inflation, the second oil price shock of 1978–1979, among others helped push the economy into a severe BOP crisis.

- An ambitious program of reform was introduced to address hyperinflation and BOP deficits while putting an end to etatist policies and institutional rigidities through an extensive program of price decontrols, interest rate liberalization, reduction of government subsidies, export promotion, and others.

o   At the same time, large incentives were provided to exporters in the form of credit, marketing assistance and others, as noted in previous sections.

-   Reforms were supported with external financial assistance and policy support from the World Bank and IMF and the economy's subsequent manufactured export performance was one of the most successful turnarounds among developing regions.
-   In 1980, a military coup followed accelerating political destabilization and rising terrorism. Subsequent attempts to forge a national consensus around the reform program included adoption of a new Constitution in 1982 followed by general elections in 1983.
-   A key feature of the reform program conducted under military rule however, was a ban on militant unions and establishment of a Supreme Arbitration Board to issue wage guidelines and wage restraint.
-   This was an attempt to overcome institutional rigidities created by Turkey's 1961 Constitution which empowered labor unions and contributed to real wage increases and inflation during the 1970s.

o   Thus, Turkey's manufactured export success was linked in part with an elite consensus consisting of financial incentives to private exporters, overcoming institutional rigidities with wage restraints together with external "push" factors in the form of higher oil prices, financial assistance from abroad, and a military coup.

References

Beblawi, H. and G. Luciani (eds.) (1987) *The Rentier State*. London: Croom Helm.

Devlin, J. (2010) *Challenges of Economic Development in the Middle East and North Africa Region*. World Scientific Studies in International Economics No. 8. Singapore: World Scientific.

Ekelund, R. Jr. and R. Tollison (1997) *Politicized Economies: Monarchy, Monopoly and Mercantilism*. College Station: Texas A&M University Press.

Hansen (1991) *The Political Economy of Poverty, Equity and Growth. Egypt and Turkey. A World Bank Comparative Study*. Oxford: Oxford University Press.

IMF (2013a) *Turkey: Selected Issues Paper*. IMF Country Report No. 13/364.

IMF (2013b) *Turkey: Article IV Consultation*. IMF Country Report No. 13/363.

Iqbal, F. (2006) *Sustaining Gains in Poverty Reduction and Human Development in the Middle East and North Africa Region*. Washington DC: International Bank for Reconstruction and Development.

Onis, Z. and J. Riedel (1993) *Economic Crises and Long Term Growth in Turkey*. World Bank Comparative Macroeconomic Studies.

Owen, R. (1981) *The Middle East in the World Economy 1800–1914*. London: IB Tauris and Co. Ltd.

Richards, A. and J. Waterbury (1986) *A Political Economy of the Middle East and North Africa*. Boulder: Westview Press.

World Bank (2000) *Turkey: Country Economic Memorandum: Structural Reforms for Sustainable Growth*. Vol. 1. Main Report. Washington DC.

World Bank (2003) *Turkey Country Economic Memorandum: Towards Macroeconomic Stability and Sustained Growth*. Vol. 1. Summary Report. Washington DC.

World Bank (2012) *Country Partnership Strategy: Turkey*. International Bank for Reconstruction and Development.

Chapter 2

Oil Markets, OPEC, and the MENA Region

In 1960, a small organization functioning more or less like a trade union was created by five oil exporting developing countries. By the mid-1970s, this organization, the Organization of the Petroleum Exporting Countries (OPEC) had grown to 12 members, the majority from the Middle East and North Africa (MENA) region and came to represent more than half of world oil exports and nearly all of the spare oil production capacity in the global economy.

With global demand for oil expected to increase from 89 mbpd (2013) to 104 mbpd by 2030, OPEC and the Middle East will remain central to the functioning of the global oil market.

This chapter explores the role of OPEC and the MENA region in influencing global oil markets. Section I reviews the state of current oil demand and supply while Section II discusses factors influencing oil price movements including the role of OPEC in oil price shocks of the 1970s, 1980s, and 2000s.

I. Emerging Trends in the Market for Oil[1]

- MENA countries hold the greater part of remaining global oil reserves with the potential to meet rising global demand for oil and are expected to produce most of the increase in global supply by the mid-2020s.
- Within the MENA region, OPEC plays a critical role in determining long-term oil supply given that more than 70% of proved oil reserves are concentrated in OPEC countries.

  o Saudi Arabia is expected to generate more than 30% of the region's total production, becoming the region's largest oil producer and exporter.
  o Other countries with large oil reserves include Iran, Iraq, and Kuwait all of which have estimated proved reserves of over 100 billion barrels.

- But there are also countervailing trends at work.
- Oil demand in developed countries has been declining since 2005 and some analysts predict that with 3–4% annual increases in fuel efficiency, demand for oil will be nearly 4 mbpd below projected levels, even without efficiency gains.

  o There are also fundamental shifts underway in the oil market. As the decline in oil use in OECD countries accelerates, demand from China is expected to overtake the United States as the world's largest oil consuming country and oil consumption in the Middle East is expected to overtake the European Union (EU) by 2030.[2]

- Recent innovations in fracking have raised estimates of world gas reserves from 50 to 20 years, with more substitution of oil for natural gas at the fuel pump.

  o About one-fifth of buses in the US already run on natural gas.

---

[1] The following discussion is based on IEA (2005), EIA (2014a, 2014b), IMF (2013), Adelman (2002), and Fattouh & Mahadera (2013).
[2] Power and water sectors will absorb a growing share of the MENA region's total primary energy use as electricity and desalinated water needs growth rapidly.

- Much will depend on the future path of oil prices.
  - o Over the long term, oil prices have fluctuated within a range bounded by low cost production in countries such as Saudi Arabia and the price of alternative fuels.
  - o Price shocks have been punctuated by physical supply and demand disruptions, compounded by financial market activity and speculation.
  - o OPEC exports about 60% of the total international petroleum trade and produces about 40% of the world's crude oil.
    - ▪ Five founding members of OPEC were Iran, Iraq, Saudi Arabia, Kuwait, and Venezuela. Today, OPEC includes Qatar, Nigeria, United Arab Emirates, Algeria, Ecuador, Angola, and Indonesia.
  - o It is integral to the functioning of the oil market.
    - ▪ Countries in the Middle East in particular, hold more than 55% of global oil reserves; 35% of which are located in Saudi Arabia alone.
  - o There is a large body of literature on OPEC's pricing power including cartel, wealth-maximizing monopolist, three block cartel (hard core, price pushers, and expansionist fringe), dominant firm, loosely cooperating oligopoly, residual firm monopolist to competitive models.
  - o Empirically, none of these models works consistently over time suggesting that OPEC's behavior has in fact changed in response to developments in the oil market.

II. What Have We Learned About the Role of OPEC in Influencing Oil Prices from Previous Price Shocks?

- Today, crude oil is consumed, stored, and widely traded with millions of barrels being bought and sold everyday at a wide range of prices agreed by transacting parties, but this was not always the case.

- During the 1950s, however, the oil market was a relatively limited market in size and scope, and oil traded inside vertically integrated companies known as the Seven Sisters.
  - Vertical integration was a solution to the inherent industry problem of having downstream refining being too risky without an assured supply of crude oil and production being too risky without an assured outlet for crude oil.
  - Multinationals controlled both upstream (exploration, development, production of oil) as well as downstream operations (transportation, refining, marketing).
  - Oil was basically traded in house through inter-company transactions with a very underdeveloped spot market.
- Oil prices from the 1950s to the 1970s were generally low and declining due to oil purchases under the Marshall Plan in which the US government financed large volumes of European oil accepting only price structures that would exist under competition.
- Prices were based on transactions between companies and were never disclosed; a posted[3] price was used as the basis for calculating royalty and income tax per barrel revenues to host governments.
  - Posted prices were usually higher than contract prices and responded little if at all to market forces of supply and demand.
  - Host governments on the other hand did not participate in crude production or pricing — they largely competed with each other to sell licenses or oil concessions.
- By the late 1950s, the oligopolistic structure of the oil market was under pressure as encroachment by "Independents" began to take effect.
  - Independent oil companies began to invest in upstream development and get access to crude oil outside the control of the Seven Sisters.

---

[3] An administered price or tax reference price.

     o The discovery of oil in Libya further increased the importance of the independents as the Libyan government chose to attract a diverse set of oil companies in addition to the majors and by 1968 independent production was about 1.1 mbpd.

- Oil concessions which originally provided for payment per unit produced were changed under pressure from host governments to 50–50 equal sharing of profits between companies and governments.

     o This began with Venezuela, followed by Saudi Arabia, Kuwait, Iraq, and Iran.

- Rising development needs necessitated borrowing by Saudi Arabia, Iran, and others as declining revenues and rising development needs created current account deficits.
- More competition for the majors was created by Iran's signing of two exploration and development agreements with non-majors in 1951 and Saudi Arabia's agreement with the Japan Petroleum Trading Company to explore and develop Saudi's fields in the Neutral Zone (which is still producing oil today).

     o While these were limited quantities of oil produced, the terms of these agreements created precedents for further negotiations by host governments to secure better terms in existing concessions.

     o Higher competition in refined products lowered prices which filtered back into lower crude oil prices.

- In response to competitive pressures, multinationals decided to cut posted prices (and thus income paid to host governments) in 1959 and 1960, catalyzing the creation of OPEC.
- In the 1970s, oil prices began to rise after nearly 25 years of steady decline.

     o Several events helped to strengthen OPEC's hand *vis-a-vis* majors in the run-up to the 1973 oil price shock.

     o In 1968, OPEC countries began pressuring oil companies for higher posted prices and thus, higher tax revenues.

o   In 1969–1970, following the Libyan Revolution and closure of the Saudi Trans-Arabian (TAPLINE) pipeline which disrupted supplies to the eastern Mediterranean prices for Libyan oil rose rapidly.

- By 1970, Libya had also negotiated an agreement with Occidental oil company, an independent, in which the company agreed to pay income taxes on the basis of increased posted prices and make retroactive payments to compensate for lost revenue since 1965.

o   This became the basis for all other companies operating in Libya and ultimately the terms for all other oil producing countries.

o   Subsequent OPEC negotiations with multinationals conducted in Teheran resulted in a collective decision to raise the posted price and increase the tax rate.

o   Abu Dhabi, Iran, Iraq, Kuwait, Saudi Arabia, and Qatar all followed Libya's lead winning a   US$0.30–0.50 increase in the posted price.

- First Oil Price Shock in 1973.

o   Factors leading up to the first oil price shock in 1973 included very rapid growth in global oil demand which was increasing at rates of more than 3 mbpd from 1965 to 1973.

o   This was coupled with a waning excess oil supply among Persian Gulf producers as Libya and Algeria priced themselves out of much of the oil market and OPEC increased shares of global crude production from 44% to 51% over the same period.

o   Production amounts more than doubled from 14 mbpd to 30 mbpd.

- In September 1973, OPEC again decided to open negotiations to increase posted prices.

o   Economic development needs were rising and many countries were in need of higher revenues to fund ambitious development plans.

o   Oil companies refused OPEC's demand for a large increase
    in the posted price and OPEC ministers walked out of the
    meeting.
o   The events following had a historic effect on the oil market.

■   On October 16, 1973 six Gulf members of OPEC unilater-
    ally declared an immediate increase in the posted price of
    Arabian Light Crude from US$3.65 to US$5.12.
■   On October 19, 1973 members of the Organization of Arab
    Oil Producing Countries (OAPEC) announced production
    cutbacks of 5% of the September volume and an addi-
    tional 5% per month.
■   In December 1973, OPEC further raised the posted price
    of Arabian Light to US$11.65.
■   This was an unprecedented and historic hike in oil prices
    creating a dramatic shift in power towards OPEC giv-
    ing the organization a more powerful role in setting the
    posted price.
■   Whereas OPEC had aimed at creating a floor under falling
    prices in the previous decade, it aimed to set the price of
    oil — a significant shift in oil market dynamics.
■   By March 1974, the embargo was lifted.

•   In the early 1970s, there were also major changes underway in
    the structure of the oil industry.

o   OPEC governments had stopped granting concessions and
    began to claim equity participation in existing concessions
    with a few countries choosing to outright nationalize oil pro-
    duction.
o   This process began in Iran in 1951, followed by Egypt in 1956
    when the government nationalized Shell's interest and by
    1963, the Syrian government had nationalized the entire oil
    sector.
o   By 1967, Algerization of oil companies had begun and by
    1970, all non-French oil interests had been nationalized; by
    1971, the government took 51% stake in French companies.

- Saudi Arabia and the other Gulf states took a slightly different approach, creating a Ministerial Committee in 1971 to plan effective implementation of equity participation.

  o OPEC's six Gulf members (Abu Dhabi, Iran, Iraq, Saudi Arabia, Qatar, and Kuwait) agreed to negotiate the participation agreement with oil companies collectively with Saudi Oil Minister, Zaki Yamani, at the helm.
  o In 1972, oil companies agreed to an initial 25% participation which would reach 51% in 1983.
  o However, only Gulf Cooperation Council (GCC) producers, Saudi Arabia, Abu Dhabi, and Qatar, signed the general participation agreement; Iran pulled out in 1972 and Iraq implemented nationalization in 1972.
  o In Kuwait, opposition from the parliament to the agreement helped push the government to take a 60% stake in the Kuwait oil company in 1964 and call for a 100% stake in 1980. By 1976, Kuwait had achieved 100% equity participation followed by Qatar in 1976–1977.

- This shift also raised additional challenges since host governments did not have access to downstream and refining markets.

  o While equity participation allowed OPEC governments to have a share of the oil produced, it was still necessary to locate third party buyers.
  o General lack of marketing experience and lack of downstream integration into refining and marketing in oil importing countries were a problem and a number of government shares of oil were sold back to the companies that held the concessions and produced the oil in the first place.
  o This created an impetus for more downstream investments in refining and marketing facilities by OPEC governments.

- A three part pricing system emerged based on posted prices, official selling prices, and buyback prices.

o Buyback prices were prices at which crude was sold back to multinationals by OPEC governments.
o It was a highly inefficient system and meant that buyers could obtain oil at different prices.
o By 1975, the use of reference or marker prices was introduced with Saudi Arabia's Arabian Light as the chosen marker crude.

  ▪ In this system, oil producing countries set Official Selling Prices in relation to the reference price, with differentials based on relative demand and supply for each crude variety and others.
  ▪ Adjustment of differentials made the process of administering a marker price more complex.

- At the same time, as multinational companies lost access to large reserves of crude oil, they became increasingly dependent on OPEC supplies.

  o It was a mutually dependent relationship since OPEC countries remained dependent on multinational oil companies to lift and dispose crude oil.
  o However, the underlying trend was a weakening of vertical integration between upstream and downstream segments of the industry contributing to development of a more open and "commoditized" oil market.
  o By the late 1970s, an increasing number of players were active in the oil market from national oil companies in OPEC countries to independent oil companies, multinationals, Japanese and independent refineries, trading houses, and oil traders.

- The second oil price shock in 1979.

  o By the late 1970s, there were other important changes underway in the oil market.
  o The quadrupling of oil prices in 1973–1974 slowed growth in demand for OPEC oil which had been growing 10%

annually for a decade and OPEC exports declined from 1973 to 1975.

- o By 1978, OPEC was forced to make its first agreement on output sharing, followed by formal fixed quotas in the 1980s.
- o Non-OPEC production was increasing although moderately between 1973 and 1978, as higher prices made development of reserves in Alaska, Mexico, and the North Sea viable.
- o Excess capacity within OPEC was rising and Saudi Arabia was forced to cut production by nearly 3 mbpd between 1974 and 1975.

  - ▪ By early 1978, spot oil prices were falling and OPEC exports had declined by 6% from the previous year.

- National development plans and ambitions within OPEC member countries were also rising.

- o From 1970 to 1978, for example, Saudi oil revenues rose 21 times, but expenditure rose 31 times from US$1.4 billion to US$43 billion and Saudi Arabia was running a budget deficit.
- o OPEC governments were also highly vulnerable to fluctuating oil revenues given that oil exports provide the majority of fiscal revenues and imports.

- According to some experts, the price changes of 1978–1979 cannot be explained entirely by insufficient supply since there was more than enough unused capacity available to offset oil supply disruptions.
- By August 1978, anticipation of a higher official OPEC price contributed to rising anxiety in the oil market.

- o A strike by Iranian oil workers in October 1978 created further fears of scarcity.
- o Expectations of higher prices were also heightened following a December 1978 OPEC meeting in which price increase of 14.5% were announced for the following year, together

with proposed cuts in production and the loss of Iranian oil in world markets.

o   An outright price panic erupted in January 1979 following the Iranian Revolution as Iranian production went off the market and heavy buying by major oil companies commenced.

o   New speculation over higher prices drove spot prices to a new high of US$39/barrel by October–November 1979.

o   By September 1980, the Saudi Official price equaled the spot price and the outbreak of the Iran–Iraq War again raised spot prices.

▪   Production levels in Iran and Iraq declined from 11 mbpd to 6 mbpd and remained at those levels until 1990.

▪   Saudi Arabia increased production and prices but trouble was brewing — by the end of 1980, OPEC exports were down by 17% since 1977.

•   The second oil price shock was exacerbated by a number of complementary factors.

o   Primary among these was the breakdown in long-term contracts for oil purchases and the growth in direct crude sales to third party buyers all of which helped to drive a buying panic.

▪   After the 1979 Revolution, Iran canceled all previous agreements with oil majors in marketing Iranian oil, while in Libya there was a shift from contract buyers including majors to new customers mainly government and state oil corporations.

▪   This set the trend for the rest of OPEC.

o   Majors who had lost access to large volumes of crude available under long term contracts along with new players expanded oil market transactions where buyers and sellers were increasingly engaged in arm's length transactions.

o Disintegration of the oil market, short term bargains, and price volatility were added to the growing commoditization of the oil.

■ Markets developed in forward sales of crude along with introduction of futures markets.

■ Refiners and marketers depending on relatively thin margins between purchase and resale prices needed to hedge against fluctuations in current prices.

— Futures markets also provided more information on spot markets.

■ Swaps were introduced as a practice borrowed from the currency market in the early 1990s.

■ All of these developments made it more difficult to maintain a price above competitive levels.

— Discounts by one seller were quickly dispersed throughout the market and lower prices on spot crude would become slightly lower prices on refined products and divert sales from some producers.

— OPEC producers fearing loss of market share would further provide discounts.

• The 1986 price collapse.

o Saudi Arabia maintained its exports at capacity at nearly 10 mbpd through 1981 which by now represented 50% of OPEC's exports.

o However, by the mid-1980s demand for OPEC oil collapsed, falling to only half its 1979 level.

o Contributing factors included OPEC's attempts to defend the 1979–1980 price doubling, global economic recession, the shift away from oil used in electricity generation and space heating and continuing growth of non-OPEC supply.

o New developments in non-OPEC countries meant that large amounts of oil reached the international market outside of OPEC primarily from the North Sea and others, with producers undercutting OPEC prices in the spot market.

- o From 1983 to 1986, non-OPEC production increased by 10 million bpd.
- o With declining demand for its oil, OPEC's market share in world oil production declined from 51% in 1973 to 28% in 1985.
- o By 1985, Saudi Arabia had cut its exports by 70% from 1981 levels to below 3 mbpd, nearly back to 1965 levels.

- Saudi Arabia is a central player in the global oil market; it accounts for 16% of global reserves and roughly 13% of global supply (1990–2011).

  - o It has about 100 major oil and gas fields although more than half its estimated 266 billion (plus 2.5 billion in the Neutral Zone shared with Kuwait) barrels of proved reserves are contained in eight fields in the northeast.[4]
  - o The Ghawar field is the world's largest in terms of production and reserves with an estimated proved reserves of 75 billion barrels.

- Saudi Arabia's oil production capacity is the largest in the world estimated at 12 mbpd in 2014 and exports of nearly 8 mbpd (2013).

  - o It accounts for over 50% of global spare capacity and the capability of raising global oil production by over 2% within 30 days, an amount equivalent to Korea's total consumption.
  - o Its spare production capacity is over 2 mbpd and the country keeps large quantities of oil in storage facilities in the Mediterranean, northern Europe, and Asia to insure against supply disruptions. Nearly 70% of crude oil exports are destined for Asia and along with most of the country's refined products.

---

[4]The Saudi–Kuwait Neutral Zone is an area of 2,230 square miles between the borders of Saudi Arabia and Kuwait. It contains an estimated 5 billion barrels of total proved oil reserves divided equally between the two countries. Crude production is about 520,000–600,000 bpd (EIA, 2014).

- o It has 23,000 miles of crude and petroleum product pipelines throughout the country and Saudi Aramco alone has 5,000 guards (in addition to 20,000 National guards protecting the pipeline network).
- o It also maintains redundancy (multiple options for transportation and export) in the oil system to enhance export security.
- o Saudi Arabia produces a range of crude oils from heavy to super light.

  - Today, more than 70% of total crude production is considered light-gravity with the remaining considered medium of heavy-gravity; oil production with the exception of Extra Light and Super Light crude oil types are sour with relatively high levels of sulfur.
  - Lighter grades of oil are produced in onshore fields while medium and heavy crudes come from offshore fields. It is currently developing new refining capacity (capacity throughput of 2.5 mbpd) and integration of crude production with large petrochemical complexes in addition to expanding overseas refining capacity (2.5 mbpd).

- Oil production in Saudi Arabia over the last 40 years reflects changing domestic priorities and global demand and supply conditions.

  - o During the 1970s, oil production tripled from 3.8 mbpd in 1970 to 10 mbpd in 1980 raising its market share form less than 7% in 1970 to 16% in 1980.
  - o By the 1980s, however, with falling global oil demand and global recession, Saudi Arabia was forced to reduce production dramatically within a system of production quotas established by OPEC.

- As several OPEC members continued to produce above assigned quotas, Saudi Arabia continue to reduce output with production falling by over 60% from 1981 to 1985.

  - o Losses of market share were necessary to defend the price of marker crude.

o   This was not sustainable however as Saudi Arabia continued to cut back production to preserve marker prices (Arabian Light) while other producers sold oil at a discount to the administered price of Arabian Light.

- By 1985, Saudi Arabia had cut its exports by 70% from 1981 levels to below 3 mbpd (21% of OPEC exports relative to nearly 50% in 1981).

  o   Exports were at 1965 levels.
  o   To address price discounting and higher production by non-OPEC members, Saudi Arabia threatened to cut prices, but with little effect on OPEC members.
  o   By late 1985, it decided to flood the oil market, adopting a netback pricing system.

      ▪   Other oil exporting countries followed and the floor dropped out from under oil prices.
      ▪   The netback pricing system allows oil companies a guaranteed refining margin even if oil prices collapse because the price of crude oil is set equal to the *ex post* product realization minus refining and transport costs.

- After 16 months of price competition and a price collapse, Saudi Arabia was able to work with OPEC to determine a new market sharing agreement.

  o   The focus within OPEC shifted from attempting to set the price and adjusting export volumes to setting production level quotas (based on assessments of market demand) and letting the "market" determine the price.
  o   Temporary agreements were reached to cut production and there was relative stability in prices at roughly US$18/barrel from 1987 to 1989.
  o   Saudi Arabia and a number of other large reserve producers (Kuwait) also began to integrate into refining markets overseas.

- After the 1986–1988 pricing debacle, OPEC pricing shifted towards a market related oil pricing system and formula pricing.

o   Beginning with Mexico market related pricing was adopted
    by most producers by 1988 and is the main method for pric-
    ing crude in international trade today.

•   1990 First Gulf War — changes in the oil market and a limited
    price shock.

o   By the latter half of the 1980s, oil consumption was rising
    strongly and production in the Soviet Union declined after
    1989.
o   Non-OPEC supply barely increased from 1985 to 1992.
o   OPEC exports increased from 12 mbpd in 1985 to 22 in 1993,
    the highest levels since 1980.
o   By 1989, excess capacity within OPEC had declined signifi-
    cantly.
o   Most OPEC countries were also trying to engage foreign oil
    companies to renew and expand old fields.

    ▪   Costs of drilling wells in the US, for example, declined
        by about one-fourth from 1984 to 1992 and 3D computer
        models were helping to enhance knowledge of old fields
        while horizontal drilling was emerging.

o   Tensions within OPEC were mounting in the form of pres-
    sures from Iraq, UAE, and Kuwait to expand quota produc-
    tion on the basis of higher spare capacity.

    ▪   Iraq began to play a more aggressive role within OPEC,
        attempting to enforce quota production on Kuwait and
        the UAE.
    ▪   Saudi Arabia signed a non-aggression pact with Iraq
        without notifying other GCC producers; Kuwait asked for
        a similar pact and was turned down. Saudi Arabia was
        under financial strain along with other oil exporters with
        high government expenditure commitments.

o   Output in excess of the OPEC quota was being sold without
    much deterioration in price, owing to rising demand.

o Experts were in fact, predicting supply shortages by 1993 and 1994.

o On August 2, 1990, Iraq invaded Kuwait; on August 5, the UN blockade of both Iraq and Kuwait commenced and prices rose faster than in previous crises to a monthly high of US$31.55 in October.

o Again, there were few physical shortages in the market due to inventory buildup and some experts estimated that there was 5 mbpd of excess capacity which exceeded the shortfall in production from Kuwait and Iraq by 1.5 mbpd.

o However, bringing excess capacity to the market required a lag.

o By September 1990, Saudi Arabia announced production increase of 2 mbpd with smaller increase in Abu Dhabi and Venezuela.

o By January 16, with the beginning of the bombing campaign to liberate Kuwait, spot prices had declined to US$27.40 and fell further to US$16.40.

o While prices had risen faster than previous episodes, the speed of the price reversal was unprecedented.

  ▪ This was facilitated in part by lack of price controls in consuming markets (1973), futures markets and the Strategic Petroleum Reserves in the US, Japan, and Germany, although these were not used.

• Following the 1990 Gulf War, however, conflict arose within OPEC as Saudi Arabia and other Gulf producers were unwilling to scale back temporary production increases.

o Within OPEC, quotas were largely suspended after the invasion and Saudi Arabia was unwilling to curtail production as it did in 1985.

o Target prices were US$18–22 per barrel.

o Between 1990 and 1992 most consuming countries also made substantial increases in taxes on oil products, roughly US$10/bbl in the EU.

o   This created a wedge between consumer and producer prices with fiscal authorities taking the benefit from lower crude prices.

o   OPEC endorsed a lower output ceiling but overproduction continued as the fiscal position of OPEC members deteriorated.

o   Only Kuwait and the UAE were still creditor nations, other OPEC nations were seeking development aid and loans from consuming countries.

• Oil Price increase in the 2000s.

o   By 1996–1998, warm winters and the East Asia recession had kept consumption growing slowly as non-OPEC production grew modestly.

o   Prices declined by over half from early 1997 through early 1999 and in March 1999 OPEC with support from Norway and Mexico agreed to coordinated production cuts.

  ▪ By mid-1999, OPEC production declined by 3 mbpd and prices moved above US$25/bbl.

o   Growth in the US and globally boosted prices through 2000 moderated in part by higher Russian production.

o   After September 11, 2001, oil prices plummeted; spot prices of WTI were down 35% by the middle of November and OPEC delayed additional cuts in production until January 2002 when it reduced its quota by 1.5 mbpd, followed by other non-OPEC producers including Russia.

  ▪ Oil prices moved back up to the US$25 range by March 2002.

o   On March 19, 2003, following the invasion of Iraq, there was more pressure on OPEC production to meet reduced production.

  ▪ Inventories in the US and other OECD countries were relatively low although US demand was increasing and Asian demand was growing rapidly.

- In 2003, supply disruptions created by security concerns, strikes in Venezuela also contributed to rising prices and US crude prices averaged US$31/bbl the highest level in two decades.
  — OPEC increased quotas to 25 mbpd to make up for the shortages from Venezuela and Iraq.
  — However, this increase was later reversed in a preemptive move to protect the oil price against the effect of rising Iraqi output and growing non-OPEC production.

o By 2004, higher oil prices were linked with supply disruptions, unexpectedly strong demand growth, particularly from China, limited, if any, growth in non-OPEC production and low spare capacity in 2004 and 2005 which was less than 1 mbpd.

- These factors are linked with crude prices in excess of US$40–50/bbl.
- China, the US, and the Middle East were all main drivers of consumption growth in the run-up to 2008.
- By 2007, OPEC members had cut back on production resulting in an inventory draw down and upward pressures on prices.
- Non-OPEC production remained concentrated in a few areas and there were production declines in Mexico, the UK, and Norway.

o Oil prices reached record highs in July 2008 in nominal and real terms with prices of Brent crude reaching US$147/bbl.

- While oil prices had been increasing steadily from early 2004, they surged by more than 150% after January 2007.
- By the end of 2008, however, oil prices had collapsed by more than 75% from US$147/bbl in July to US$36/bbl in December 2008.
- By June 2009, they had recovered to US$70/bbl.
- From 2003 to 2008, OPEC's total spare capacity remained near or below 2 mbpd or less than 3% of global supply,

providing little cushion for fluctuations in supply in a context of rapidly rising demand.

- There was no net increase in annual production in non-OPEC from 2005 to 2008.
- Some analysts claim that the price run up and decline prior to 2008 were also particularly exacerbated by formation and collapse of an oil price bubble.
- More rapid recovery in Asia in 2009 helped to boost prices again in 2010, along with improved economic growth.
- Prices surged from US$70/bbl in December 2009 to US$80.29/bbl in January — the highest levels since 2008.
- Global recovery for most of 2010 with growth of 4.32% further boosted oil prices.

o By 2011, geopolitical events in the MENA region helped boost oil prices to US$103–123/bbl.

- For the first time ever, the annual average nominal price of Brent went above US$100 to stay at US$111/bbl.
- In 2012, prices increased further as supply disruptions in the North Sea and West Africa sparked fears of tensions and increased speculation in crude futures markets.

o Oil price increases in the latter 2000s were one of the largest in the history of oil prices with analysts pointing to a failure of production to increase between 2005 and 2007 rather than short-term supply disruptions.

o Global demand was growing strongly, particularly from China which increased consumption by 870,000 barrels a day, higher than two years earlier.

o This surge in demand, together with rapidly rising costs outside OPEC and financial market activity all likely sustained oil price increases at unprecedented levels.

References

Adelman, M. (2002) World Oil Production and Prices 1947–2000, *Quarterly Review of Economics and Finance*, 42(2): 169–191.

Fattouh, B. and L. Mahadeva (2013) *OPEC: What Difference Has it Made?* Oxford: Oxford Institute for Energy Studies.

International Energy Agency (2005) *World Energy Outlook: Middle East and North Africa.* Chapter 4. Paris: OECD.

International Monetary Fund (2013) *Saudi Arabia: Selected Issues.* Washington DC.

US Energy Information Administration (2014a) *Annual Oil Market Outlook.* Washington DC: US Department of Energy.

US Energy Information Administration (2014b) *Saudi Arabia.* Washington DC: US Department of Energy.

Chapter 3

Oil, the Macroeconomy, and Growth in the MENA Region

In the brief period from 1970 to 1974, government revenues of Organization of the Petroleum Exporting Countries (OPEC) nations increased 11 times and OPEC developing countries gained pricing power over the world's most valuable traded commodity.[1] This oil windfall, followed by two others (1979/1981 and 2003) had significant effects on growth, development, and political economy in the economies of the Middle East and North Africa (MENA) region.

However, by the mid-1980s and 1990s, the majority of oil and hydrocarbon exporting countries were in the midst of a growth collapse, rising external indebtedness, and high unemployment.

How did this happen? This chapter explores the link between oil wealth and development in the context of the MENA region. Section I surveys mechanisms for managing oil revenue windfalls, including the use of stabilization and savings funds. Section II concludes with a discussion of the role of oil in development in the context of two MENA oil exporting countries: Kuwait and Algeria.

---

[1] The following is based on Karl (1997), Lederman & Maloney (2007), Devlin (2010), Gelb (1988), World Bank (1965, 1971, 1989, 1994), IMF (2001, 2005, 2008, 2009, 2011, 2012, 2013, 2013a, 2013iv) and Planning Board (1970).

I. Managing Oil Revenues in the Developing Country Context

- The key to managing volatile oil prices is to smooth expenditures over time by encouraging a lagged response of government spending to oil windfalls.

  o This means that governments must effectively de-link current spending levels from current oil revenues smoothing expenditures across time.

  o But this also implies that the government will save all or part of the windfall during the upswing and reduce assets to maintain expenditure during the bust.

- How can governments including those in MENA countries achieve this? Many have turned to a combination of policy instruments including stabilization and savings funds, fiscal rules, and industrial policy measures.

  o Stabilization and Savings Funds — a stabilization fund is intended to combat volatility and budget shortfalls whereas a savings fund is for intertemporal purposes.

  o Political economy factors also play a role in a country's decision to establish a stabilization and savings fund. This has to do with limited capacity to absorb funds productively (particularly in small economies such as Kuwait) and governance.

  o A well-designed oil fund with appropriate checks and balances can help to improve transparency in oil transactions, particularly on the revenue side. In some cases, it can also improve the quality of expenditure.

  o However, it is important to point out that a stabilization fund cannot in and of itself stabilize the real exchange rate.

    ▪ Volatility of the real exchange rate is caused by volatile expenditure patterns. Smoothing expenditures over time with the help of a stable fiscal policy implies the use of a fund as governments accumulate and decumulate assets as prices or volumes rise and fall.

- A fiscal rule can help to de-link current expenditures from current oil prices and is typically based on an estimate of permanent income or sustainable revenue as opposed to transitory revenue.

  o The structural revenue rule (used in Chile), for example, is designed to smooth spending and provides a way to save part of the windfall income or spend part of the accumulating savings during temporary declines in income. It can restrict overspending with higher than expected prices but does not clearly indicate whether the amount saved or spent is optimal, given oil production profiles, volatility, and others.

  o In the Permanent Income Hypothesis (PIH) model, spending is smoothed by computing an annuity value that can be consumed forever based on a net present value of oil wealth. According to PIH, transitory shocks to oil prices should have no impact on spending. Permanent income (or wealth) is the maximum amount that can be spent in perpetuity. Thus, if a government adopts this rule, then it will achieve both savings and stabilization objectives. It addresses intergenerational equity concerns but does not deal with income volatility and is sensitive to parameters such as the real interest rate, oil prices which project far into the future.

II. How well have MENA Countries Managed Oil Revenues? Algeria and Kuwait

(a) Algeria

- Prior to independence, the Algerian economy was highly dependent on France with nearly one million Algerians employed in France, mostly as construction and factory workers and nearly one million French colonials and other Europeans living in Algeria.
- Following an eight year war of independence, Algeria became a republic and French colonials left the country *en masse* creating disruption.

○   This exodus created a sudden shrinking of the modern sector with investment and consumer demand declining and initial paralysis in public administration and heavy unemployment which threatened political and social stability.

•   The new government grew out of the revolutionary movement, chose a one party system and a reconstruction of society along socialist lines.

○   During the 1960s, under Ahmed Ben Bella, Algeria launched a development program focused on promotion of light industry especially consumer goods and agrarian reforms.

•   Development policies aimed to raise output and living standards, narrow income disparities between groups and regions, and consolidate economic independence. This was implemented with a strategy of heavy industrialization in the context of a centrally planned economy with a dominant public sector.

○   Relative to other developing countries and those in the MENA region, Algeria's economy developed in a highly centralized way with extensive state control and a system of fixed and administered prices.

•   Industry grew as a result of nationalization, high levels of investment, and price interventions.

○   During the colonial period, Algeria's industry was almost completely owned and operated by private foreign interests. Industry was heavily concentrated in a few large cities, mainly Algeria, Oran, and Constantine.

○   Following independence, these industries were nationalized with electricity, mining, and manufacturing (besides hydrocarbons) coming under the control of national companies, self-managed enterprises, and other public enterprises.

▪   Some public industry included mixed companies with majority participation by the public sector such as Air Algeria.

○   National companies were monopolies and tended to dominate manufacturing, energy, and mining activities, whereas self-managed companies were concentrated in construction materials and food production.

o Private enterprises were generally small and clustered in textiles, shoes, and leather production, generating about 30% of private industry.

- From the mid-1960s through the 1970s, policies shifted dramatically with the accession of Houari Boumediene and adoption of heavy import substitution industrialization policies and extensive state controls.

  o Under Boumediene development policy focused on (Hirshmann-type) heavy industrialization and growth poles through promotion of industries with backward and forward linkages such as heavy producer goods industries (steel, fertilizers, and petrochemicals) and creation of new industrial centers in locations such as Annaba.

  o Following the influence of Samir Amin, the economy also became close to global trade based on the view that dependence was linked with export goods and luxury consumer goods.

    ▪ Trade took place through official channels only, imports were controlled and foreign exchange was tightly allocated.

  o The industrial strategy thus focused on import substitution with public enterprises playing the major role in the industrialization process.

  o Regionalization of investment helped locate heavy industrial projects in the interior of the country although the location of several large scale projects bore little attention to market and factor availabilities resulting in high investment and operating costs.

    ▪ Lack of industrial experience in the regions and delays in establishing supporting infrastructure were serious obstacles. Low capacity utilization plagued industry for years to come and was linked with lack of skilled manpower, limited management capacity, difficulties in supplying

intermediate goods and spare parts resulting from rigidities in the system of import monopolies and import procedures. This was compounded by lack of incentives and
production efficiency.

- All prices and formal wage scales were administratively determined and public enterprises and soft budget constraints were
instituted similar to Eastern European countries.
- The state also had a virtual monopoly on allocation of invest-
able resources through control over the banking system and
direct investments.
- Agriculture was the dominant export sector before the discovery and expansion of oil production although the sector faced
challenges with a dual mode of production between modern
and traditional sectors.
  - Algeria is the second largest country in terms of land area in
  Africa and the 10th largest in the world.
  - Agricultural cultivation included a modern sector located in
  the fertile plains and operated initially by the French producing wines, citrus, and vegetables and contributing about
  60% of total agricultural output.
  - The traditional sector on the other hand located primarily in
  the north was characterized by more basic cultivation techniques and concentrated on extensive livestock raising and
  cereal production.
  - Most farms were small (less than 20 ha) but an estimated 5,000
  relatively large private holdings (more than 100 ha) represented less than 1% of total farms but occupied about 15% of
  private agricultural land.
    - Very little government support was provided to the pri-
    vate, traditional sector.
  - Most agricultural production was marketed through official
  agencies at prices determined by the government, particular in the self-managed sector, while the private sector was
  required to follow these channels with the exception of marketing fruits, vegetables, and meat.

○ Policies during the 1970s focused on reorienting agricultural exports towards import substitution with the aim of sufficiency in cereals and creating employment opportunities.

  ▪ Cereals accounted for nearly 90% of annual crop production.
  ▪ Throughout the 1970s, output fluctuated considerably, while climactic conditions and production failed to keep pace with population and rising consumption levels.

• Oil and gas were considered the leading sector of the economy supplying energy as well as raw materials for other industries such as electricity, refining, fertilizers, chemicals, plastics, and whose growth would create a major source of demand for the products of other industries and services such as steel pipelines, household durables, transport, and distribution.

○ In addition to its proximity to European markets, Algeria's oil resources benefited from technical qualities similar to Libyan oil, mainly low density and the virtual absence of sulfur. Oil output grew by an average rate of 10.5% per year between 1963 and 1970.

○ However, reserves were limited and Algeria focused increasingly on diversification within the hydrocarbon sector to develop natural gas export potential.

  ▪ With some 10% of world gas reserves in the 1970s, field discoveries in northern central Algeria were some of the largest known fields in the world.
  ▪ In the oil sector, the government gradually assumed greater control.

    — Sonatrach, created in 1963, grew steadily until by 1970 it controlled half of all activity in the hydrocarbon sector and had a dominant role in exploration and domestic distribution. By 1980, it controlled all oil production compared to 1963 when foreign administrators and technicians in the hydrocarbon sector had outnumbered Algerians by nearly four to one.

- Between 1975 and 1980, Sonatrach was implementing 27 macro projects each with a capital cost of more than US$100 million, more than any other country in the developing world. By 1983, Algeria had the world's largest LNG export capacity and gas was being piped to Europe under the Mediterranean Sea via the Straits of Messina.

- Annual population growth during the late 1960s and 1970s was over 3% and there were high rates of rural urban migration with the urban population increasing from 33% to 41% of the total population.

  o Nearly 60% of the population was under 20 years old, causing extremely rapid growth of demand for housing, urban facilities, education and social services, employment and food.

  o Improvements in social indicators were dramatic.

    - Primary and secondary enrollment rates increased from 57% and 6% in 1969 respectively to 90% and 25% in 1978 despite extremely rapid growth in the school age population.

    - Ratios of population per physician declined from 8,600 in 1965 to 1,200 in the late 1980s while infant mortality fell from 154 per thousand to 6 per thousand.

- Half a million new jobs were created during 1974–1977 mostly in services (50%), industry and construction (40%).

  o Agricultural employment was still high estimated at 40% of the workforce in the late 1970s although the labor surplus in rural areas was diminishing somewhat as a result of regional industrial enterprises and other regional development programs.

  o Employment (non-agricultural) increased by 6% per year during the 1970s, with the civil service absorbing about two-thirds of new jobs.

o Average labor productivity grew modestly — about 2% per year during the 1970s in industry and decreased by 1% per year in services.

- The first oil price increase created a domestic oil windfall of 22% of non-oil GDP from 1974 to 1978, peaking at nearly 40% in 1974.

  o More than 80% of this was allocated to public sector investment, mostly capital intensive projects with investment reaching 72% of non-oil GDP by 1977.
  o Public investment programs were about twice as large (relative to the non-oil economy) as in comparator countries and capital intensity was two to three times higher.
  o Algeria also augmented the windfall by extensive foreign borrowing suggesting that it was in fact an extremely resource constrained economy.

- The economy was becoming increasingly dependent on oil and exhibiting some symptoms of the Dutch Disease (DD).

  o By the early 1960s, half of Algeria's exports came from oil increasing to about 75% of export earnings by the early 1970s.
  o Despite very high rates of investment, real GDP increased by only 6% per year in the 1970s.
  o Although agriculture still supported half of the population by the early 1980s, agriculture and (non-oil) manufacturing had expanded only modestly and were about 20% smaller than the norm for countries at similar levels of per capita income.

    ▪ The construction sector expanded from 13% to over 20% of GDP between 1972 and 1981.
    ▪ Real wage increases were initially moderate but became substantial particularly in agriculture after 1976.

- In 1978, the economy shifted gears again as Bendjedid Chadli assumed the presidency with less emphasis on capital accumulation and central planning.

- o The focus in development policy shifted towards social and infrastructure investment along with greater consumption and a slowdown in investment.

- However, pressures were mounting. Shares of investment in GDP remained high at over 40% until the early 1980s, one of the highest levels in the world.

  - o These high investment levels however were paired with low levels of capital efficiency.

    - During the 1980s, Algerian industry had Incremental Capital Output Ratios (ICORs) of around 12, about twice the level of most middle income developing countries.

  - o Time lags for competition of large public industrial investments were long and new industrial plants were running substantially below capacity.

- Despite very high rates of investment, per capita GDP growth was modest and unemployment remained high.

  - o Annual growth in per capita GDP was about 3% during the 1970s, 2% through the first half of the 1980s and −2.2% from 1986 to 1992.

- Agriculture continued to languish and during the early 1980s, despite large investments in the state farm sector, Algeria was importing food equivalent to 80% of value added in agriculture.

- By the mid-1980s hydrocarbons accounted for 97% of export earnings and 44% of government revenues.

- Wealth accumulation became more concentrated and issues of equitable distribution of oil rents came to the foreground.

  - o To address this, a complex system of taxes and subsidies was established creating various price distortions and exploited by operators on the black market. Shortages of goods occurred.

  o Large inflows of petrodollars going to the Central Bank and negative real interest rates together with an abundant money supply drove a large wedge between official and black market exchange rates with the effect that the price of the dinar was five times higher on parallel markets than the official rate.

- In the mid-1980s, the oil shock reduced terms of trade by 50% and increased budget deficits, forcing the government to adopt stabilization measures.

  o Per capita revenues fell from US$1,200 in 1981 to about US$200 in 1986. In response, the government cut imports by 35% and raised non-hydrocarbon taxes as well as reduced current and capital expenditures.

  o In 1987, government expenditures were further reduced, living standards declined rapidly and real consumption per capita declined by about 8% in 1986 and 1987.

  o Continuous depreciation of the real exchange rate and limits on public spending and borrowing helped stabilize the macroeconomy by the late 1980s.

  o In 1988, efforts to break the direct link between the Treasury and productive firms included privatization of state farms and establishment of autonomous public enterprises and banks, including reform of the incentive system, interest rates, commodity prices, and increased flexibility in allocation and price setting.

- A new Constitution was introduced in 1989 stipulating separation of the government from Parliament, an independent judiciary, freedom to form associations, and new emphasis on the rights of private ownership.

  o The word socialism disappeared from the new Constitution.

- Reforms were reversed however in 1992/1993 following the launch of a civil war, lower oil prices, and rapidly expanding external debt.

o   Trade and payment restrictions were tighter, the fiscal deficit reached 9% of GDP and the dinar appreciated by nearly 50%.

o   By the end of 1993, Algeria was unable to meet external debt commitments, inflation was approaching 30%, and official reserves fell to two months of import cover.

o   By mid-1994/1995, the economy had stabilized with a near 100% devaluation of the currency, elimination of non-tariff trade and exchange restrictions, maintaining a budget surplus and reduced subsidies on energy and food products.

o   Government wages were capped and credit limits imposed on public enterprises along with introduction of a privatization law and modernization of commercial and investment codes.

o   The banking and insurance sectors were opened to private investment and a social safety net system was introduced based on self-targeted public works, a means tested program for the elderly and the handicapped, and an unemployment insurance scheme.

• By the late 1990s, the economy had stabilized and Algeria had substantially reduced external debt obligations, but the supply response to macroeconomic and structural reforms was disappointing.

o   A 1998 referendum to amend the 1989 constitution was passed and Abdul-Aziz Bouteflika became the President.

o   By the late 1990s, the civil war had claimed the lives of some 100,000 civilians and numerous political figures.

o   GDP continued to decline and the economy remained heavily dependent on hydrocarbon exports which accounted for 95% of exports, 60% of government revenues and one-fourth of GDP.

o   Manufacturing was contracting in the face of more foreign competition and open unemployment was approaching 30% of the labor force.

   ▪ The overhang of more than 2 million unemployed slowed further progress on privatization of public enterprises.

- o While a large number of public enterprises were liquidated, limited private sector activity was largely confined to small scale and informal trade and rent seeking activities.
- o Public sector activity continued its *quasi*-monopoly in manufacturing, finance, housing, transport, mining, and utilities sectors making it difficult for the private sector to compete in these sectors and limiting global competitiveness.
- o Trade and foreign exchange liberalization without growth in private sector development and a productive sector dominated by the non-competitive public enterprises created deindustrialization and weak integration into global markets.
- o The decline in real wages, rising unemployment, and civil unrest weakened further progress on deeper reforms in banking, manufacturing, housing, and agriculture.

- • Following a decade of near zero growth in per capita income in the 1990s and very low investment, a rebound in oil prices in the 2000s helped the Algerian economy turn the corner.

- o By the 2000s, Algeria was the sixth largest producer of natural gas in the world and the value of oil and natural gas exports increased from US$24 billion in 2003 to nearly US$80 billion in 2008 and US$56 billion in 2010.
- o In 2004, Abdelaziz Boutelflika was reelected and put forth the Charter for Peace and National Reconciliation endorsed by a referendum in late September.
- o Development policy priorities shifted from structural, market-oriented reforms toward delivery of services to citizens (social housing, education, water, energy, and health) through increased public investments and social transfers.
- o Financial wealth accumulated from hydrocarbon exports has followed two main principles: centralization of risk management at the Central Bank and investment in foreign assets typical of central banks.

  - ▪ Hydrocarbon earnings go directly to the Central Bank and are part of international reserves with a small liquid portion and a large portfolio of high grade fixed-income securities.

- A unit within the Central Bank manages the fund according to benchmarks set by the authorities and returns on reserves are transferred to the budget in the form of Central Bank dividends.
- Thus, the Fund for the Regulation of Receipts (FRR) is a subaccount of the government at the Central Bank in dinars and lacks governance arrangements and investment goals of sovereign wealth funds used by other large commodity exporters (i.e., Norway).

  ○ Massive increases in public investment followed higher oil prices with a US$55 billion public expenditure program in 2005–2009 and investment rates increased significantly during the second half of the 2000s reaching nearly 50% of GDP in 2009.
  ○ Algeria also became a net creditor during the 2000s, reducing external debt from 41% of GDP in 2001 to 2.8% of GDP in 2010.

- Despite the dip in oil prices in 2008/2009, the government did not scale down public investment and financed expenditures including raising salaries of civil servants without resorting to the FRR.

  ○ By 2009, the public investment program represented half of public spending (46%) followed by personal expenditures (21%) and social transfers (19%).
  ○ An estimated 70% of the Public Investment Plan (PIP) was allocated to housing, infrastructure, irrigation, and education projects.
  ○ Manufacturing contracted, particularly in textiles and food processing activities.
  ○ Imports increased rapidly reaching nearly US$40 billion in 2008 relative to US$18 billion in 2004.
  ○ Algeria weathered the 2008 financial crisis and declining oil prices by drawing down foreign exchange reserves and current expenditures increased 31% in 2010 due to public salaries (new hiring of about 60,000 civil servants) and higher

wages together with higher maintenance costs associated with infrastructure.
o Expansion plans for Sonatrach further buoyed domestic demand.

- Following protests in January 2011 in conjunction with the Arab Spring, the state of emergency in place, since 1992, was lifted and actions were taken to quiet popular discontent.

  o An estimated 50% increase in current expenditure was linked with price support for food staples (cereals, powdered milk, soybean oil, and sugar) expanded civil service salaries, better access to housing for civil servants and increased support for mechanisms to reduce youth unemployment including support to small and medium-sized enterprises (SMEs).
  o Inflation peaked at nearly 9% in 2012.
  o President Bouteflika won a fourth term as President in 2014 and fiscal policy has been increasingly focused on social and job support policies together with higher civil service salaries.

- Average annual growth during the 2000s was 3.5% (2004–2008) although very uneven across sectors;

  o Growth was fastest in sectors such as services, construction, energy, and water sectors.
  o Inflation remained moderate reaching 6% in 2009 and declining thereafter.
  o However, reform of state-owned enterprises and privatization made little progress during the 2000s as did regulatory simplification, reform of the commercial legal framework and state-owned bank reform.

    ▪ In 2004, the public sector's share of value added in non-oil industry was 63% mainly in construction materials, chemicals, metallurgy, and paper together with owning 90% of financial institutions by assets and the largest employer, representing about 34% of total employment.
    ▪ SMEs provide 10% of jobs and the SME sector in Algeria is two to seven times smaller than in competitor countries.

- ▪ Moreover, previous measures in favor of trade and investment openness have been reversed to reduce dependence on imports and strengthen local economic actors.
- ▪ Foreign direct investment (FDI) flows were less than 1% of GDP in 2012.

  — New policies include a 49% ownership limit by foreign investors for all new FDI projects, obligation of every FDI project to maintain a positive foreign exchange transfer balance over the life of the project making it less profitable for an investor to locate in Algeria unless it exports a significant share of production, preferential treatment to local firms in public procurement and others.

- In 2011, the economy was still heavily dependent on hydrocarbons which represented 98% of export revenues and more than two-thirds of government budgetary revenues.
- Financial intermediation remains low with the banking sector remaining very liquid with relatively low lending due to high credit risks.

  o Measures to improve intermediation during the 2000s included increasing minimum capital requirements for banks and insurance companies, raising bank limits to invest and promoting mortgage and loans to SME financing with government incentives.

  o However, progress has been limited and new consumer lending restrictions introduced in 2009 are expected to negatively affect intermediation.

- Social indicators also improved in the 2000s relative to the 1990s although unemployment remains high.

  o Life expectancy increased from 53.5 in 1970 to 74 years in 2008 and access to health facilities is 98% of the population.

  o Fertility rates declined radically from 4.6 births in 1990 to 2.4 in 2007.

o Algeria performs better than most countries in the region in gender parity of health indicators. Social safety nets remain generous but not as effective as intended.

■ Algeria ranks 104th among 182 countries in terms of the UN Human Development Index.

o Per capita spending on health and education between 2000 and 2011 doubled in real terms.

o Inequality declined as the Gini coefficient fell from 0.34 in 2000 to 0.31 in 2011 although the Gini coefficient of rural households was twice that of urban households.

o Algeria virtually eliminated extreme poverty and poverty is heavily concentrated in rural areas affecting an estimated 10.5% of the population in 2008.

■ Poverty incidence is highest among people in mountainous areas in the northern part of the country and in the Southern Sahara region.

o While unemployment dropped significantly over the 2000s, it remains high among youth, women, and educated workers.

■ Falling from nearly 30% in 2000, unemployment was 10.2% in 2009.

• With hydrocarbon prices below US$45/bbl current policies would be difficult to continue highlighting the need for a fiscal rule to de-link current expenditures from current oil prices.

o Public spending alone cannot guarantee future growth. Reforms have mainly focused on assessing the impact of the PIP on current spending and developing tools to enhance program performance and better control spending.

o What is needed, however, is to direct fiscal policy to a long term sustainable path which could be gauged against rules derived from the permanent income framework.

o The current fiscal framework allows fiscal savings to accumulate in the oil savings fund (FRR) based on a budgeted oil price of US$37/bbl, although there is no limit to the withdrawal of funds to finance spending and no limit on the fiscal balance.

○ One criteria would be to maintain a constant real wealth or constant real wealth per capita over the medium term.

○ An appropriate fiscal rule would target the primary fiscal balance consistent with long term sustainability and establish a limit on drawings from the FRR.

○ A PIH rule would help to ensure fiscal sustainability by requiring that the constant non-oil deficit equal the implicit return on the present value of future natural resource revenue. An alternative rule is to combine a backward looking five year oil price formula with a 5% floor on the structural primary balance and a cap on drawings from the oil savings fund.

(b) Kuwait

• Kuwait has the sixth largest proven oil reserves in the world with a per capita income of nearly US$50,000 in 2012. Similar to the period of the 1960s, oil accounts for 95% of exports and 63% of GDP, and 85% of total government revenues (2011).

○ While oil was discovered in the late 1930s, it was not commercially exploited until after World War II and by the mid-1960s Kuwait was fourth among the world's crude producers and second only to Venezuela as an oil exporter.

• Over a period of a few decades, Kuwait was transformed from a small town of traders, fishermen and Bedouin to a modern welfare state with one of the highest per capita incomes in the world for a number of years.

• During the 1960s and 1970s, the size of Kuwait's oil wealth was unprecedented with annual oil income reaching US$300 million by the mid-1950s when the population was less than 200,000.

• Thus, unlike most developing countries, Kuwait faced the challenges of development with a high capital surplus — gross savings were estimated between 40% and 50% of GDP from 1959 to

1968 and an estimated US$300 million in capital was exported given limited investment opportunities in the city-state.

o   But an abundance of capital does not solve the development problem, and in the case of Kuwait was complemented by scarcity of other factors namely non-oil natural resources, skilled, and unskilled labor.

• Nearly all consumption and investment goods and labor had to be imported and Kuwait had one of the highest levels of per capita import levels in the world at more than US$800 in the late 1950s and 1960s.

o   By the late 1960s, reliance on imports remained high since most of the local manufacturing industry was concentrated in fabrication, processing, and repair activities.

o   Local production focused initially on production of bread, soft drinks, lime cement bricks, and cement products of which imports would be prohibitively expensive.

o   Labor — both skilled and unskilled — came from developed countries as well as other Arab countries, Iran, Pakistan, and India.

• By the mid-1960s, diversification and creation of a more diversified and balanced economy was a primary development objective as stipulated in the First Five Year Plan and nearly every subsequent planning document.

o   A Planning Council was created in 1962 to help spearhead the effort and formation of the National Assembly in 1963 (Kuwaiti Parliament) also played a role.

o   Diversification by necessity focused on industrial development given weak prospects for agriculture or trade.

■   However, the small size of the local market and limited resources were also a barrier to development of industrial capacity.

o   Petroleum refining and fertilizers were important industries developed during the 1960s and 1970s. Unlike other oil producing countries, Kuwait went further in investing and building up "downstream" oil production and distribution capacity.

- Among others, it developed a chain of European gas stations operating under the "Q8" logo.
  - Government support for industrialization included contributing half or more of the capital for most of the large industrial enterprises, developing a large industrial estate and supporting small scale industries.

- The economy was completely dependent on oil revenues which had been increasing by about 8% per year during the 1960s.

  - However, unlike Algeria, only half of foreign exchange earnings were used for commodity imports whereas nearly one-fifth was invested abroad by the Government and about 32% was used for foreign private investment or remitted abroad by the private sector. Earnings from the Government's foreign assets were also reinvested abroad.
  - Reserves were accumulated in the General Reserve Fund and the Reserve Fund for Future Generations. Created in 1960, the General Reserve Fund absorbed budgetary surpluses with discretionary transfers to the budget in the event of budget shortfalls. In 1976, the Reserve Fund for Future Generations was established as a savings fund which accumulates 10% of government revenues for investment in overseas financial assets. Transfers from the fund remain discretionary to the budget with approval by the National Assembly.

- In addition to a high rate of savings, Kuwait was able to maintain a very open economy for imports and financial remittances. However, restrictions on foreign investors and workers remained high.

  - Customs duties were low, averaging 4% *ad valorem* duty.
    - Today, tariff rates are slightly higher given that Kuwait applies GCC tariff rates but income taxes only apply to foreign investors.

- Import licenses mainly in the form of import monopolies granted by the government helped to expand large trading conglomerates in Gulf society.

o Despite openness to trade and foreign companies, investors faced high income taxes and requirements to work with a Kuwaiti partner with a controlling interest.

- Income taxes for foreign investors were 50% of total net income with income exceeding KD375,000.
- Moreover, the total exclusion of foreign investors from entering into new insurance and banking ventures was considerably more restrictive than practices in competitor countries.

o While labor immigration was encouraged and by the 1960s migrant labor represented nearly half the population and two-thirds of the work force, naturalization laws were very restrictive. Much of this holds true today.

- In the case of labor compensation, despite high levels of labor imports, high wage policies of the Government which employed about one-third of the labor force artificially raised the wage structure economy wide.
- Today, Kuwaitis represent about 32% of the total population of about 3.8 million and the labor market is highly segmented. About 70% of government employees are Kuwaitis while 95% of private sector employees are non-Kuwaitis.

- For most of the 1970s, oil represented well over 60% of GDP and 90% of merchandise exports and stimulated the growth of some private sector activity and large government activity.

o Fiscal surpluses accumulated for much of the 1960s with most of the distribution of oil revenues to the private sector implemented through large scale land purchases and some increase in current expenditures.

- Relative to other GCC states, land purchases were an extremely important form of oil revenue distribution in

Kuwait with beneficiaries concentrated among the mer-
chant elite and tribal notables.

- Government investment in industry was limited and a
  small number of industries were established primarily
  producing construction materials which benefited from
  high transportation costs and large expenditures by the
  government.

• Growth in government also accompanied higher oil revenues.

  ○ Prior to the discovery of oil, the government in Kuwait and
    elsewhere in the GCC was extremely limited.
  ○ Nevertheless with the growth of oil revenues came a rapidly
    expanding state apparatus.

    - By the late 1960s, there were an estimated 19 ministries
      and after the 1970s, these structures ballooned rapidly. In
      Kuwait, the size of the civil service more than doubled
      between 1966 and 1976 and then increased by another
      25% in 1983.
    - By 1988, some 42% of citizens held jobs in the civil
      service, not including employees of the Central Bank,
      public institution for Social Security, a number of gov-
      ernment sponsored research agencies, Kuwait Air-
      ways, Kuwait Petroleum or other government-owned
      corporations. These figures do include the military.

• Free healthcare, free education, subsidized housing as well as
  grants, low interest and no interest loans from small business to
  getting married to building a home all necessitated higher levels
  of government services and were all provided to the national
  population.

  ○ Social security pensions to the aged, widowed, divorcees,
    and the disabled were also established along with extensive
    subsidies on consumer goods and public services.

    - Bread, rice, sugar, flour, and meat prices were either
      controlled by the government or subsidized by the

government or both. State sponsored cooperatives in Kuwait have provided food products at subsidized prices.

- Gasoline is sold by state marketing companies at prices well below international levels.
- Water, electricity, and telephone services are provided either free of charge or at subsided prices.

- Government expenditures closely followed oil prices and were highly volatile in the 1980s and 1990s.

  o Real consumption per capita was relatively flat during the 1990s along with lower oil prices.

- However, unlike other MENA countries such as Algeria, reserve accumulation in part helped Kuwait to weather the downturn in oil prices during the 1980s and the economy did not experience a severe decline in growth.

  o There were limited efforts at privatization during the 1980s with Kuwait selling most of its shares in 10 state-owned companies and divesting in 4 others.

- Growth during the 1990s languished with the exception of the acceleration after the invasion until the early 2000s.

  o Moreover, it was more volatile, given the drawdown in reserves associated with the reconstruction following the Iraqi invasion.

  o In 1992, for example, the Kuwait government forgave all telephone, water, and electricity bills accrued during the crisis and suspended the current costs to consumers of those services.

    - All government employees were paid in full for the period of the occupation. Under pressure from the National Assembly, the government also agreed to provide each Kuwaiti family that remained in the country the equivalent of US$1,750.

  o By the mid-1990s, expenditures on wages, salaries, and domestic transfers were nearly 30% of GDP in the mid-1990s compared to 23% during the late 1980s.

o Higher government spending put rising pressure on fiscal balances as lower investment income became a reality due to the significant drawdown in foreign assets associated with reconstruction.

• Nevertheless, Kuwait's downstream oil and gas industries continued to perform strongly.

o The sector expanded by 9% in the 1990s relative to the 1980s and increased shares of GDP from 1% in 1982 to 5% in 2003.

o Plans for further investment in the 2000s have included US$30–40 billion over the next 15 years to rehabilitate refineries, add new refineries and increase oil production capacity to 4 mbpd by 2020 from 2.5 mbpd.

• Real GDP grew at 3% per year after the mid-1980s and at 2% per year after the mid-1990s until the 2000s.

o Reforms in the 1990s were aimed at accelerating non-oil growth, financial, and monetary stability and maintaining intergenerational equity.

o Core elements of the reform program included reducing the role of the public sector, promoting private investment, deepening and widening of the financial sector, reform of the labor market, and expenditure restraint.

o Actions implemented were selective, however, given difficulties in reaching political consensus between the government and parliament as well as regional uncertainties.

▪ Selective reform measures included divestiture of shares by Kuwait Investment Authority (KIA) equivalent to about 12% of GDP in 2001 as well as 30–50% increases in domestic petroleum product prices in 1999.

▪ Health insurance and related charges were levied on expatriate workers.

▪ KIA also divested shares acquired after the Suk Al Manakh crisis of 1982.

▪ While the law on privatization languished in the National Assembly, private investors were encouraged to invest in areas where explicit approval by the National Assembly was not required, notably telecommunications, health, and education.

- Financial sector liberalization also occurred in the 1990s with the limitation of administrative ceilings and floors on various categories of deposits and loans.

- During the 2000s, growth accelerated and Kuwait has been running large budget and current account surpluses over the 2000s. The economy however is increasingly dependent on oil revenues.

  o Kuwait's government expenditure as a share of non-oil GDP was 77% in 2011.

    - A 10% increase in oil prices tends to directly increase non-oil GDP growth by 0.8% points.

    - Moreover, oil related subsidies and benefits constituted 20% of government expenditure in 2011 and tend to increase with economic growth and associated higher consumption, population growth, and the increase in global oil prices as retail prices are fixed and not revised frequently.

    - In 2011, following the advent of the Arab Spring, the Amir also granted a cash transfer of US$3,600 to each Kuwaiti citizen (equivalent to nearly 3% of GDP in 2010) and the provision of free essential food items from February 2011 to March 2012.

  o Thus, growth in the 2000s has been driven by higher government expenditures including the public wage bill and investment which was largely concentrated in services (about 20% of GDP) and transport (6% of GDP).

    - Public sector employment for nationals increased by about 7% between 2005 and 2011 at double rates of the 1990s and the public sector wage bill more than doubled from 2006 to 2012. This also puts longer term pressure on government finances through wage increases, pension contributions, and an increase in unfunded liabilities of the pension system.

- Manufacturing and trade tended to grow more slowly than comparator countries.
- In 2010, a four year development plan was launched which is the first in a series of plans based on a strategic vision for 2035 emphasizing investment in infrastructure, health, and education and coparticipation by the private sector through establishment of public shareholding companies. It also aims to diversify Kuwait into a regional financial and trade hub.

• Kuwait also made tangible progress on structural reforms, with the National Assembly passing laws on foreign portfolio investment, FDI, and components of labor market reform.

   ○ Thus, foreign investors could now own and trade shares of joint stock companies listed on the Kuwait Stock Exchange (KSE).

   ○ In total, foreigners may not own more than 49% of the capital of a particular bank except with the recommendation of the Central Bank of Kuwait (CBK) and approval by the Council of Ministers.

      - The new FDI law allows foreigners to own 100% of Kuwaiti companies subject to conditions determined by the Council of Ministers.

   ○ Under the labor market reform bill, the number of children entitled to an allowance has been limited to five (previously there was no limit).

      - A social allowance was also extended to Kuwaitis in the private sector and unemployment benefits paid to Kuwaitis seeking employment in the private sector.

• However, investment remains low, relative to comparator countries and the case of Algeria.

   ○ Kuwait has a low investment rate relative to comparators and levels of competitiveness and investment slowed considerably in the post reconstruction period (1997–2003).

o Moreover, much of this has been public investment, which was one and a half to twice the size of private investment in the 1980s although declined to about one half to one third after the mid-1990s.
o This argues in favor of a fiscal rule.

■ The IMF estimates that using a social planner's life cycle optimal consumption and investment model, Kuwait's current spending in the 2000s is higher than optimal and investment is too low.
■ Moreover, a 1 dollar decline in permanent income should reduce consumption by 0.45 cents and investment by 0.20 cents and precautionary saving by 0.35 cents. According to this model, the optimal investment rate is 20% of permanent income, initial consumption is 50% and savings is about 30%.

References

Devlin, J. (2010) *Challenges of Economic Development in the Middle East and North Africa*. Singapore: World Scientific.

Gelb, A. (1984) *The Oil Syndrome: Adjustment to Windfall Gains in Oil Exporting Countries*. Development Research Department Discussion Papers. No. 94. World Bank.

Gelb, A. (1988) *Oil Windfalls: Blessing or Curse?* Oxford: Oxford University Press.

Karl, T. (1997) *The Paradox of Plenty*. Berkeley: University of California Press.

Lederman, D. and W. Maloney (2007) *Natural Resources: Destiny or Curse?* Washington DC: World Bank.

Nashashibi, K. (1988) *Algeria: Stabilization and Transition to the Market*. Washington DC: International Monetary Fund.

IMF (2013) *Kuwait: Article IV Selected Issues*. Washington DC.

IMF (2005) *Kuwait: Article IV*. Washington DC.

IMF (2005a) *Kuwait: Selected Issues and Statistical Appendix*. Washington DC.

IMF (2008) *Kuwait: Article IV*. Washington DC.

IMF (2009) *Kuwait: Article IV*. Washington DC.

IMF (2001) *Kuwait: Article IV*. Washington DC.

IMF (2003) *Kuwait: Article IV*. Washington DC.
IMF (2011) *Kuwait: Article IV*. Washington DC.
IMF (2012) *Kuwait: Article IV*. Washington DC.
World Bank (1971) Economic Development and Prospects in Algeria. Washington DC.
IMF (2011a) *Algeria: Article IV*. Washington DC.
IMF (2013a) *Algeria: Article IV*. Washington DC.
World Bank (1965) *The Economic Development of Kuwait*. Washington DC.
World Bank (1989) *Country Assistance Strategy for Algeria*. Washington DC.
World Bank (1994) *Algeria: Economic Reform Support Loan*. Washington DC.

Chapter 4

Water Scarcity in the MENA Region

Managing water resources pose significant challenges for policymakers globally — the amount of water readily available for human use is less than 1% of total water resources in the world.

Water resource scarcity is particularly severe in the Middle East and North Africa (MENA) — the most water "poor" region in the world where per capita water resources have declined by 60% since the 1970s. In Yemen, for example, groundwater tables in the Sana'a Basin are falling by as much as 6 m per year and government officials are considering moving the location of Sana'a, the capital city.

This chapter surveys underlying factors driving water scarcity in the MENA region and explores policy approaches to more sustainable water management. Section I discusses rising water scarcity in the context of the MENA region and underlying contributing factors. Section II explores policy approaches to more sustainable water resource management with a focus on specific countries in the region.

- Water is a renewable resource but finite.

  o The amount of water readily available for human use is less than 1% of total water resources in the world.[1]

---

[1] Globally, freshwater resources are scarce — an estimated 70% of the Earth's surface consists of water, but the majority of it, that is, 96% is saline. Of the remaining

II. Water Scarcity in the MENA Region[2]

- In the MENA region, ensuring access to freshwater resources for activity and human welfare is particularly challenging. Globally, between 1950 and 2030, it is estimated that per capita water resources will decline by 60%. In the MENA region, water resources per capita have already declined by 60% since the 1960s.

- Today, countries in the MENA region are among the most water scarce globally with per capita freshwater availability well below a global water "poverty" line of 1,000 cubic meters per day.

- Contributing factors to MENA's growing water scarcity include

  o An arid environment;
  o Climactic factors including decreased water availability due to more episodes of drought and declining rainfall;
  o Inadequate groundwater and surface water replenishment and pollution;
  o Rising water demand (population, income).

- Arid conditions, low, and variable rainfall and high rates of evapotranspiration[3] all affect the region's water availability.

  o Rainfall in arid environments tends to be highly variable and this is also the case for most MENA countries.[4]

4%, an estimated 70% is trapped in ice caps and glaciers with the remainder consisting of groundwater. Moreover, there is only so much water available in any given location, and actions in one part of the hydrological system have large effects on other parts (US Geological Survey, 2011).

[2] The following discussion is based on World Bank (2006, 2007), Brooks (1996), Strategic Foresight Group (2011), Hammer (2013), Elhadj (2004), Easter (1992), Saghir *et al.* (2000) and Jagannathan *et al.* (2009).

[3] Evapotranspiration is the amount of water that is lost from water and vegetation surfaces with little or no economic gain.

[4] Where water surpluses occur across the MENA region, they tend to be concentrated in northern areas, i.e., northeastern Turkey, the mountains surrounding the Black Sea and Mediterranean coasts of Turkey, and coastal uplands of Syria and Lebanon.

- In Jordan, for example, over 90% of the country receives less than 200 mm of rainfall per year and annual rainfall varies from 50 mm in the eastern and southern desert regions to 650 mm in the northern Highlands.

o Unpredictability and concentration of water resources has contributed to vast investments in water storage and dam capacity with a focus on supply side management.

o In Jordan, for example, rainfall is highest in the Northern and Southern Highlands, where most of the country's rivers originate and 90% of the population lives in Northern areas. Whereas 80% of the country receives less than 100 mm/year of rainfall, amounts of water in these highland areas can be as much as 600 mm/year.

o Most of Jordan's larger dams are thus located in this region.

o More generally, an estimated 90% of surface freshwater resources are stored in reservoirs in the MENA region, compared to less than 20% in Sub-Saharan Africa and 10% for global averages.

o However, despite such huge investments, in water storage capacity, many countries in the region use less than 60% of total dam capacity.

- Iraq in particular has some of the largest dams in the region with a combined capacity of over 50 BCM. Dams in Mosul on the Tigris and the Haditha Dam on the Euphrates hold nearly 20 BCM and can irrigate a combined area of three million ha of land.

• Droughts are also common and costly in terms of economic output and poverty incidence.

o During the mid-1990s, for example, episodes of drought in Morocco were linked with a 45% decline in agricultural output and loss of 100 million work days for rural landless workers and small landholders.

o A recent episode of drought in Syria from 2006 and 2011, is estimated to be one of the worst in modern history and displaced an estimated 1.5 million people.

- ▪ According to the UN, about half of the population in Syria between the Tigris and Euphrates Rivers migrated to urban areas contributing to social tensions and political instability.
- • Water scarcity is likely to worsen with climate change.
  - ○ Experts predict changes in climactic patterns may result in shrinking of rivers, desertification, receding groundwater levels, and shifting rainfall patterns.
  - ○ Summer temperatures are expected to rise by 2.5–3.7°C and winter temperatures by 2–3°C over the next 50–70 years contributing to faster evaporation of surface water.
  - ○ Precipitation is expected to decrease on average by 5% by 2100 and there are already droughts in Israel, Jordan and the desertification and decreasing groundwater levels in Syria and Iraq.
    - ▪ Approximately 60% of the land area in Syria faces a threat of desertification.
- • The region has limited surface water supplies.
  - ○ Only three rivers are considered large by world standards, the Nile, Euphrates, and the Tigris.
  - ○ All three face challenges with reduced flow and rising pollution levels.
  - ○ Satellite images from the Gravity Recovery and Climate Experiment reveal that the Tigris Euphrates Basin is losing water faster than any other place in the world, except northern India, with the loss of 117 million acre feet of stored freshwater between 2003 and 2009.
  - ○ In addition, pollution in the Tigris River caused by the discharge of drainage water from agricultural areas and sewage discharge near Baghdad, for example, is a major constraint to freshwater availability in Iraq.
- • There is also high dependency on water resources crossing international borders.

o Jordan, for example, shares most of its water resources with other countries, as in the case of the Jordan River with resources shared across Israel, Jordan, Lebanon, and Syria.

o Each riparian has traditionally undertaken separate and partial planning with resulting piecemeal development of the river.

• Groundwater aquifers are critically important but pose particular challenges.

o Globally, groundwater accounts for nearly 30% of the world's freshwater and is one of the most important and vulnerable sources of water.

▪ It is usually higher quality and better protected from direct pollution, less subject to seasonal and perennial fluctuations and more uniformly spread over large regions of the world than surface water.

▪ In Jordan, for example, groundwater aquifers contribute about 33% of total freshwater resources, 60% in Israel and 100% in the West Bank and Gaza.

• Aquifers found in the region occur in two types: shallow and deep.

o Shallow aquifers occur along river valleys, unconfined, smaller in area and have water tables which respond to local precipitation conditions.

▪ This is considered to be a renewable "groundwater" resource in that aquifers are recharged by rainfall and river flow, primarily during spring and early summer.

▪ However, overpumping, saltwater intrusion, and pollution through use of chemical fertilizers and industrial activities as well as urban development are all factors contributing to rapid deterioration in shallow aquifers.

▪ Using more than the stipulated safe yield makes aquifers susceptible to saltwater intrusion and waste materials from the soil.

- o Deep rock aquifers are less permeable and usually made of sandstone and limestone which are confined systems and hold water which can be thousands of years old.
  - However, recharge rates are so low (estimated to be 5 mm/year in semi-arid areas such as Texas) that these water resources can be considered practically non-renewable.
- o Most groundwater users do not pay a "resource" charge for groundwater use, contributing to overexploitation and contamination.
  - In Jordan, groundwater resources are spread across 12 major basins, 10 of which are renewable aquifers and two located in the southeast are fossil aquifers.
  - About half of the shallow aquifers are being overexploited and in some cases, annual withdrawals of groundwater are more than 100% of annual safe yields.
  - In Saudi Arabia, agricultural development policies adopted since the 1980s are linked with an estimated depletion of two-thirds of the country's "fossil" water supplies or deep water aquifers.
- o Estimates of national wealth consumed by overextracting groundwater are equivalent to nearly 2% of GDP for Jordan, Yemen, Egypt, and Tunisia.
  - Energy subsidies, in particular, enable the transfer of surface water across large distances and pumping of "fossilized" groundwater.
- Despite the region's scarce water resources, water demand has grown rapidly with population and income and today, countries such as the UAE currently consume twice the global average level of per capita water.
  - o Per capita consumption is 550 L per person, relative to 250 L per day on average globally.
- Agriculture still accounts for the lion's share of water use in the MENA region.

o   Globally, agricultural accounts for 70% of all water withdrawn, across the MENA agriculture accounts for on average 85% of freshwater use.

   ▪ In some countries, such as Syria, allocations are even higher during the 2000s, for example, agriculture accounted for 95% of total water withdrawals compared to just 3% for domestic use and less than 2% for industrial use.

o   MENA countries have some of the largest irrigation networks in the world, effectively "locking" in agricultural water use.

   ▪ Iran, for example, houses the fifth largest irrigated area in the world and water requirements can be very large — for gravity irrigation schemes, water resource requirements are equivalent to a city of 1 million people on peak days.

   ▪ Water losses are also high, estimated at 60% in some areas due to inefficient irrigation and domestic water supply networks in Syria, for example.

o   In most MENA countries, irrigation water is priced below cost.

   ▪ When combined with energy, fertilizer, credit subsidies, and price supports, such subsidies artificially raise the marginal value product of irrigation water.

   ▪ Relatively small price increases do not necessarily offset the incentives provided by crop prices and other subsidies.

o   Agricultural policy has protected water intensive crops and in many cases lower value drops such as cereals and grains under the auspices of food security (Saudi Arabia), supporting poor farmers (Morocco and Tunisia) and protecting employment.

   ▪ In practice, however, such measures have proven to be very costly in terms of output and water resources and have concentrated benefits among certain groups, primarily large farmers.

- ■ Public sector support for cereals, legumes, and pulses in Tunisia is estimated to cost four times per capita GDP every year for each job protected.
- ■ Moreover, protests in Morocco in 2005 were focused on policies of regional irrigation offices which gave priority water allocations to sugar beet and fodder crops leaving little water remaining for other crops.

- Urban water allocation accounts for about 10–15% of the region's water and public sector utilities are inefficient with estimated water losses of over 30%.

  ○ This is high relative to international best practice of 10%.
  ○ Residential consumers pay relatively higher prices for water and most connection fees are subsidized.
  ○ Cost recovery remains a problem. On average, 58% of residential tariffs have no cost recovery with 25% of residential water tariffs covering partial operation and maintenance (O&M) costs and 16% partial capital costs.
  ○ Moreover, water losses are high with an estimated 35% of lost water to faulty infrastructure and bad pipes.

    ■ Levels of unaccounted water in Lebanon are even higher at 40% of the total water supply and 60% in Syria.
    ■ There are growing shortages of water in urban areas with water supplied about twice a week in Amman during the summer and once a month in Taiz, Yemen.

  ○ Social equity concerns are a factor given that households are forced to purchase water from private vendors charging between 3 and 14 times more than public providers for same volume of water.
  ○ Moreover, rural areas face particular hurdles. In the mid-2000s, for example, an estimated 56% of the rural population in Morocco had access to improved water supply and sanitation services.

- Water policy and planning tends to be fragmented across institutions and organizations.

o It is frequently the responsibility of ministries of irrigation (Jordan, Egypt, Syria) agriculture (Bahrain, Tunisia) energy or electricity (Kuwait, Iran, Saudi Arabia) or planning or environment (Morocco, Oman, Yemen).

o Algeria has a dedicated Ministry of Water although it is not responsible for water supply and sanitation.

o In many cases, ministries are responsible for both service delivery and regulation of the quality of service, although in some countries, operations and regulation have been separated (Jordan, Morocco, Tunisia).

III. Policies to Enhance Sustainable Water Use in the MENA Region

• MENA countries have undertaken a number of reforms to improve the efficiency of water use including (i) more efficient pricing and reduced water use in agriculture, (ii) augmenting supplies through investments in large scale desalination and reuse of treated wastewater, (iii) promoting water saving education and technologies and (iv) improving water institutions and governance and more engagement with the private sector.

o In Morocco and Tunisia, for example, governments have introduced volumetric pricing for public irrigation, charging farmers by the amount of water they use rather than hectares under cultivation.

  ▪ Tunisia's irrigation policy led to total recovery rate of 115% of operation and maintenance costs by 2000.

  ▪ In Morocco, a formula-based system was introduced in 1984 in which volumetric tariffs are directly linked to supply costs and governments relaxed crop pattern regulations to induce more efficient water use. Irrigation charges almost completely cover operations and maintenance in Tunisia.

  ▪ There is also increasing willingness by farmers in Egypt and Morocco, to pay tariffs for full cost recovery for reliable, good quality water services for high value export crops.

- In Jordan, reforms have included introduction of a progressive block tariff and metered water supplies in irrigation.

o High value crops are expanding, albeit slowly along with economy-wide and trade reforms.

- The growth of high income, modern horticultural producers such as Egypt's Western Delta, and the Jordan Valley will all have an impact on agricultural policy and water resource use.

— Citrus dates, horticulture, nuts, tomatoes, apples, all offer higher returns to land and water than field crops.

— Value added per cubic meter of water is about US$0.37 for vegetables, rising to US$0.75 for fruits.

— Moreover, high value export crops also generate more employment than traditional crops such as cereals.

⇒ Horticulture in Morocco, for example, requires nine times more labor than traditional cereal farming.

- Nevertheless, many MENA countries are not achieving export potential in high value fruits and vegetables.

— From 1990 to 2003, fruits and vegetables increased shares of total agricultural output by weight from 20% to 26% and growth in shares of cropped area from 10% to 13%.

— Morocco, for example, has the potential to dominate total European Union (EU) tomato imports but in the mid-2000s exported only 60% of the available quota. Much of this has to do with low productivity in agriculture.

— In Tunisia, citrus orchards are old and less productive with low yields and fruit that are too small to get good prices.

⇒ Harvesting practices are also problematic since fruits which are tree harvested and those collected on the ground are often mixed together with fruits of all quality levels and sizes sold together.

o In Tunisia, PNEEI National Program of Irrigation water conservation, a water saving program, was introduced equipping 305,000 ha or 76% of all irrigated areas with water saving technology.

▪ This increased water-use efficiency from 50% in 1990 to 75% in the mid-2000s.

o Water governance and institutions have improved management through even greater community involvement in planning processes and water policy in Egypt, Jordan, Morocco, Tunisia, and the West Bank and Gaza.

▪ In general, such organizations are most engaged in Morocco and least engaged in the Gulf Cooperation Council (GCC) countries. In Egypt, on the other hand, there are more than 270 environmental non-governmental organizations (NGOs), but few have strong grass roots linkages to influence policy.

▪ Other organizational changes include proliferation of Water User Associations in Egypt, Iran, Jordan, Morocco, Oman, Tunisia, and Yemen to enhance irrigation management.

— In Yemen, such organizations have had some success with improving irrigation services and modernizing irrigation equipment.

— In Egypt, when cultivation patterns switched from one crop per year prior to building the Aswan High Dam to perennial irrigation and increased crop intensity (200%) problems of land salinization and waterlogging emerged.

⇒ The government played an important role in developing innovative subsurface drainage mechanisms (which did not take up much land area) and created the Egyptian Public Authority for Drainage projects within the Ministry of Water Resources and Irrigation which acted flexibly and rapidly to address the problem including full cost recovery for drainage investments.

⇒ At the time, Egypt was one of the few countries worldwide which had developed institutions with capacities to address drainage needs.

o River Basin Management Agencies are also playing a role.

- Morocco has the longest experience in the region with river basin agencies which were established by law in 1995.

- Algeria has established five river basin agencies and Yemen has devolved regulatory responsibility to the regional level through branch offices of the National Water Resources Authority.

o Countries in the region have also passed new water law legislation:

- This includes modern water laws in Morocco (1995), Yemen and West Bank and Gaza (2002), whereas others have published water resource management strategies including most of the Gulf states.

o Water markets in irrigation are evolving on a small scale to improve water resource management.

- In Bitit, Morocco, for example, farmers trade water rights with water allocation rules being clear and transparent, and based on the *Frida*, that is, a detailed, publicly available list of all shareholders and their water rights expressed as hours of full flow.

  — However, the system is not property regulated and prohibits selling irrigation water for non-irrigation purposes.

- In Yemen, on the other hand, farmers may purchase water from nearby well owners or purchase tanker water to apply to high value crops.
  - Costs are large and farmers are charged more than US$1/cubic meter if the crop is *Qat*.
  - In Taiz, a fleet of private tanker lines up at the wells around the city that have been converted from agriculture to water supply and domestic and industrial consumers pay tanker owners for supplies delivered to their doors.
  - However, these are generally informal and opportunity markets with a limited number of potential buyers and sellers are not transparent, contributing to price gouging and lack of regulation of water quality.

- In Morocco, urban water supply has been enhanced with the introduction of private sector concessions for water supply and sanitation services in a number of large cities.
  - This concession is regulated through the Delegating Authority which determines tariff caps, service standards, priority projects, and investment obligations.
  - The Authority has also required private operators to extend the water network to low income households using a work fund which is financed by the cities' network access fees and 0.5% of tariff revenues.
  - Rules and guidelines for adjusting tariffs have also been introduced including a price cap requiring that any tariff increase of more than 3% be made in agreement with the government.
  - The government also retains the ability to make unilateral changes to tariffs in the public interest as long as it compensates private operators for losses.
  - Water is now available 24 hours a day in these four cities and water supply connections have increased by

almost one-third since the concession began. In
addition, tariffs increased three fold, a sanitation
charge was introduced and reduced leakages have all
acted to reduce demand by 3%.

- In Tunisia, on the other hand, urban water supplies are
  publicly owned and operated along with sanitation services.

  — The *Society National d'Exploitation de Distribution des
  Eaux* (SONEDE) is responsible for domestic and
  industrial water supply in all urban areas.
  — It is regulated by the Ministry of Agriculture, Environment
  and Water Resources, has financial independence, a
  predictable set of tariff increases and a clear set of
  performance standards. Coverage is universal, water is
  available 24 h per day and losses are relatively low.

(a) MENA Country Experiences — Jordan

- Jordan is an extremely water scarce country and one of the
  fourth driest countries in the world.

  o Annual per capita water availability has declined from about
    3,600 cubic meters per year in 1946 to 145 cubic meters per
    year in 2008.
  o This is less than one-third of the widely recognized water
    poverty line.

- The country has an estimated 104 mm of average precipitation
  per year, highly irregular distribution of rainfall throughout the
  year and large variability of yearly precipitation.

  o The coefficient of variation ranges between 30% and 45%.

- Evaporation largely exceeds precipitation and the streamflow of
  wadis and rivers is intermittent.

- Surface water supplies contribute about 37% to Jordan's total
  water supply while the majority of water resources are sourced

by groundwater which contributes about 54% to total water supply.

o The Yarmouk River is the largest source of fresh surface water in Jordan but has been declining from about 375 million cubic meters 40 years ago to less than 100 million cubic meters at present.

• Water demand far exceeds available supply with an estimated 64% going to irrigation, 30% for municipal use, 5% for industrial use, and 1% for tourism.

o Municipal and industrial water users compete increasingly for the same groundwater resources as agriculture, particularly in the highlands east of the Jordan Valley.

o Rationing of municipal water that is serviced to the population twice a week has become more frequent.

o At the same time, value added by each cubic meter of water used in industry was US$7.95 compared with only US$0.20 in agriculture.

o In addition, each 1,000 cubic meter of water generated 13 times more employment in industry than agriculture.

• Water projects accounted for about a third of all public investment during the 1990s and together with subsidies to support water management activities are more than 3% of GDP.

o Forward-looking projections suggest even larger shares will be needed — as much as US$250 million per year or about 3% of GDP.

• Groundwater contributes most of Jordan's total water supply and is currently being exploited at about twice its recharge rate. About 10 out of 12 water basins are overpumped, and

o Unsustainable abstraction is due to population growth and agricultural expansion together with lax enforcement of regulations on private sector drilling and the near absence of controls on licensed abstraction rates.

- As water tables drop, pumping costs and salinity levels are increasing.
- Jordan's 2008–2022 Water Strategy proposes measures to address these, including

  - Establish groundwater basin user associations to help set and protect zones of surface and groundwater.
  - Improve monitoring and metering of groundwater quantity and quality.

    — Jordan's Groundwater Law 85 was created to protect and monitor the country's groundwater resources and under this law, the government has responsibility to collect fees for legal wells.

    — However, fees from the majority of wells used for agricultural purposes are not collected and hundreds of illegal wells pump water daily.

    — The bylaw also requires the government to establish appropriate pumping reduction plans for aquifers under stress.

- Jordan also shares both surface and groundwater resources with neighboring countries.

  - A large fossil groundwater aquifer too deep for economic exploitation except in the south of Jordan at Disi is an example.
  - The Upper Yarmouk shallow groundwater aquifer is over-exploited by farmers upstream and municipalities which are all competing for the same water.

- Agriculture which contributes about 3% of GDP uses about two-thirds of water resources.

  - Only about 6% of Jordan's land is arable and production of food in semi-arid countries is largely impossible without irrigation.

    - Irrigated agriculture provides the majority of agricultural production and jobs.
    - However, dry land farming is used on about half of this potential area because of volatile rainfall. About 8,000 more

ha remain to be irrigated north of the Dead Sea and some 2,000 ha south of the Dead Sea.

▪ Agricultural cultivation in the highland areas is based on groundwater resources and led by the private sector with some 44,100 ha under cultivation.

— Irrigation practices in the highlands are not controlled and irrigation efficiency is poor.

○ Heavy agricultural subsidies, low water tariffs and import restrictions provide few incentives for more water efficient and higher productivity irrigated agriculture.

▪ In 1995, the Jordan Valley Authority (JVA) increased the water tariff 2.5 times and adopted an increasing block tariff structure but average tariffs remain very low.

— Moreover, in 1997, the tariff declined by 10% as JVA tried to offset adverse impacts of water shortages on farm incomes by forgiving or delaying collection as a form of social relief.

▪ In the mid-2000s, average JVA tariffs (1995–2000) were US$0.008 per cubic meter while amounts collected averaged US$0.006 per cubic meter.

— In 2001, however, urban water tariffs were about 90 times higher at US$0.54 per cubic meter. Industrial and non-residential users were charged even more — US$1.54 per cubic meter.

— Studies suggest that if agricultural water were valued at average urban tariffs, the implicit annual agricultural subsidy would be US$200 million or US$3,200 per ha.

▪ Treated wastewater effluent is added to the water stock used for irrigated agriculture and is contributing a rising percentage of irrigation water. However, all JVA water, including poorer quality recycled water is charged the same, causing resentment among farmers because of the limited range of crops feasible with recycled water.

- Evidence for the West Bank and Gaza which also has similar agro-climactic conditions and well-developed export
  markets suggest that farmers are willing to pay US$0.20
  for almost all crops, but when water charges are raised
  to US$0.60 per cubic meters, only cultivators of orchards,
  niche vegetables and flowers are willing to pay these rates
  for fresh water.
- In Jordan, gross profits are high for most tree crops and a
  number of vegetables and the cost of water as a production input has been relatively low compared with gross
  profits generally. The additional cultivation of irrigated
  banana areas in the Jordan Valley in spite of high-water
  costs (17% to 29% of gross profits) also suggests that even
  modest returns are acceptable (2000–3000 JD/ha or about
  US$2,800–3800/ha).

• Political economy factors play an important role in water
pricing.

  ○ To address inefficient water pricing, policymakers have pro-
    posed administrative allocation of water rather than higher
    water prices.
  ○ With an estimated net cost of US$3.5 million per year of pro-
    viding water to the Jordan Valley and sustain livelihoods
    for some 300,000 people, the Government of Jordan (GOJ)
    considers this to be a relatively small amount compared
    with the social costs incurred if very high water charges
    caused farmers to abandon land and migrate to Amman for
    employment.
  ○ In the highland areas, farmers have been able to withdraw
    groundwater without billing despite the introduction of wa-
    ter monitoring devices and an official policy to charge for
    water.

    - According to the GOJ, highland farmers already pay a
      high cost for well installation and pumping whereas those
      in the Jordan Valley have water delivered to the farm gate
      by the JVA.

- Powerful agricultural lobbies have played a role and irrigated areas in groundwater dependent highlands increased from 31,000 ha to over 40,000 between 1996 and 2000 with the majority of acreage planted in tree crops which have a higher priority in water allocation.
- According to the 2002 Groundwater Management Policy, priority is given to the sustainability of existing irrigated agriculture where high capita investment have been made.
- Moreover, cultivators of fruit trees are seen as having higher social status than farmers of field crops because of assured prices of water and tend to be more financially secure.

- Higher water tariffs did not necessarily reduce agricultural water use given other political and administrative factors.

  o Water allocation decisions by JVA on the basis of water availability and quotas are calculated from crop types with first priorities given to perennial crops (citrus and fruit orchards, followed by bananas).

  - Residual water is then distributed to vegetable farmers.

  o Areas under citrus and banana cultivation have thus expanded rapidly despite the fact that they use two to five times more water than vegetables.

  o While vegetable crops are not individually as profitable as citrus crops, with good management crops can be planted two or three times per year and make similar profits.

  - This provides more risk-averse production relative to reliance on a citrus monocrop and allows seasonal adjustment to water shortages.
  - It is also more labor intensive with high employment and social benefits.
  - At present, vegetables appear to exhibit high water-use efficiency — nearly all cultivation is under high-tech irrigation.

- On the other hand, about 90% of orchards have not adopted drip irrigation and most use basin irrigation.
- Water rights continue to reside with the government.
  - While all water is state owned, the rights of traditional and private use are implicitly recognized and allowed.
  - Allocating water rights to all farmers and allowing them to be traded could provide better incentives for water efficiency improvements.
- Low domestic prices and high risks associated with export markets provide disincentives for agricultural investments.
  - Jordan's production capacity is much higher than export capabilities and risks associated with export markets have also dampened irrigation technology and efficiency improvements.
  - With a small local market, there is an inability to absorb growing agricultural output.
    - Irrigated tomato production, for example, increased by 50,700 tons between 1990 and 2000 while exports only increased by 22,000 tons which lowered local prices.
  - Production, marketing, and logistics are not well aligned with export opportunities and the GOJ is undertaking measures to address this.
  - GOJ aims to address this by providing incentives for farmers to grade agricultural produce by quality, sort by size and conformity and practice proper post-harvest handling and transport increasing agricultural product quality and lengthening shelf life.
    - This would help allow farmers to focus on high quality crops with the potential for higher profits and resources to upgrade technology and pay higher water tariffs.
    - In addition, the GOJ has emphasized the need to remove tariffs on imported crops to promote transition to crops with higher economic returns per unit of water used.

— Banana cultivation is a commonly cited example of a crop that can be imported significantly more cheaply than it can be produced in Jordan.

- Ongoing plans to improve the efficiency of water use in agriculture include

  o Jordan's 2008–2022 Water Strategy proposes a number of measures to address these issues including:

    ▪ Reducing the annual water allocation for irrigation in the Jordan Valley and in the highlands as well as developing more efficient bulk water distribution and more efficient on farm irrigation systems.
    ▪ Improving policy to equitably allocate transferable surface and groundwater rights to farmers to permit intra- and inter-sectoral transfers of water.

      — Jordan Valley farmers would thus know in advance their allocation of the crop season and plan accordingly.
      — Farmers could sell part or all of their surplus annual water rights to other farmers.
      — In addition the GOJ is considering possibilities to buy highland groundwater rights at market prices to reduce withdrawals from aquifers under stress.

  o Treated wastewater is to be used for activities demonstrating the highest financial and social returns including irrigation and other non-potable uses.
  o Transition to one service provider for irrigation water with more private participation and farmers associations involved in the retail function for irrigation water.
  o Moreover, appropriate water tariffs and incentives will be introduced along with alternative technologies such as rainwater harvesting.

- Developing additional sources of water

  o Currently treated wastewater is generated from 21 wastewater treatment plans used primarily for irrigation in the Jordan

Valley. Most of Amman's treated wastewater is discharged in the Zarqa River and stored in the King Talal Dam where it is blended with fresh surface water and subsequently released for irrigation use in the Jordan Valley.

o Elsewhere treated wastewater is discharged in rivers where it represents a significant portion of the stream flow since most streams in Jordan carry very little water.

o Higher population growth and increased water use is creating increasing pressure for treated wastewater.

o Desalination is very energy- and capital-intensive and costly for a country such as Jordan.

- Given current water tariffs, the necessary subsidies would place a heavy burden on the national budget.

- Plans are underway to desalinate brackish and sea water as well as use wastewater treated effluent in highest social and economic return uses.

• Municipal demand is growing rapidly with service levels at 97% of the population in urban areas and 83% in rural areas.

o Urban water demand is expected to almost double by 2020 while agricultural use is expected to remain the same.

o To address this, the GOJ has planned a 13 year US$2.5 billion investment program to boost supplies and service efficiency.

o Urban wastewater disposal also pollutes or degrades existing surface water, thus constraining its use.

o High service efficiency in urban areas has been helped by new investments in water supply together with the transfer of water from the Jordan Valley through the Deir Alla pipeline.

o Municipal water management also suffers from unsustainable subsidies and staffing levels, inadequate water tariffs and high unaccounted for water.

- Unaccounted for water in municipal networks is high and estimated to be about 50%.

- Institutional challenges for water resource management loom large.

  o Jordan's water resources are managed across three entities — the Ministry of Water and Irrigation (MoWI) created by a "bylaw" and the WAJ and JVA, both of which were created by laws.

  o There are conflicts of interest in addition to overlaps with responsibilities of other ministries.

    ▪ Communication among the three entities is limited with each functioning in near isolation with and in competition with the other.

    ▪ A top-down approach is typically applied and stakeholders are not normally involved in the decision-making process.

    ▪ Overstaffing of MoWI, WAJ, and JVA are a problem and there has been an exodus of skilled staff to the private sector.

  o JVA, originally the Jordan Valley Commission was established in 1973 based on the model of the Tennessee Valley Commission and was renamed the JVA in 1977. Its responsibilities cover irrigation, power, land improvement, social development, planning and development of towns and villages including tourist infrastructure.

    ▪ It has full managerial and operational control of water in structure down to the farm level, while municipalities are in charge of other civil works.

    ▪ JVA has a monopoly on the Valley which limits the Ministry of Agriculture's extension activities in the region.

    ▪ The JVA is running a deficit; losses were estimated to be an average of US$6.8 million per year in the 1990s and early 2000s.

  o The WAJ has oversight of all existing water supply and sewerage operations including municipal water supply demand of the JVA and 300 municipalities and villages.

- Moreover, WAJ's focus on urban water supplies means it has paid little attention to upland irrigated agriculture. There is also a need to devolve more of WAJ's activities in distinct geographic areas to local level management.
- It is regarded primarily as an urban water agency but also has regulatory oversight of 56% of Jordan's groundwater based irrigation in upland areas east of the Jordan Valley.
- WAJ remains heavily reliant on subsidies despite restructuring to unbundle bulk water and retail activities and water supply and wastewater services.

o The Ministry of Water and Irrigation created in 1988 oversees both the JVA and WAJ, but they have remained semi-autonomous with financial and administrative independence with their own employees.

- Attempts have also been made to rationalize the organization of the MoWI and its line agencies to improve water management.
- This included, for example, absorbing WAJ's resource studies and groundwater monitoring functions.

o In the late 1980s, a National Water Master Plan was introduced along with efforts to improve central water administration, develop guidelines for water policy and create a computerized water sector data bank and an integrated water sector management model.

References

Brooks, D. (1996) Between the great rivers: Water in the heart of the Middle East in *Water Management in Africa and The Middle East: Challenges and Opportunities*, E. Rached, E. Rathgeber and D. Brooks (eds.), p. 75. Ottawa: International Development Research Centre.

Easter, K. W. (1992) Intersectoral water allocation and pricing in *Country Experiences with Water Resources Management: Economic, Institutional, Technological and Environmental Issues*, G. Le Moigne, S. Barghouti, G.

Feder, L. Garbus and M. Xie (eds.). World Bank Technical Paper No. 175. Washington DC: World Bank.

Elhadj, E. (2004) Camels Don't Fly, Deserts Don't Bloom: An Assessment of Saudi Arabia's Experiment in Desert Agriculture. Occasional Paper No. 48. School of Oriental and African Studies/King's College London. University of London.

Hammer, J. (2013) Is a Lack of Water to Blame for the Conflict in Syria? *Smithsonian Magazine*, June.

Jagannathan, V., A. Mohamed, and A. Kremer (eds.) (2009) *Water in the Arab World: Management Perspectives and Innovations*. Washington DC: International Bank for Reconstruction and Development.

Saghir, J., M. Schiffler, and M. Wodu (2000) *Urban Water and Sanitation in the Middle East and North Africa Region. The Way Forward*. Mimeo. World Bank.

Strategic Foresight Group (2011) *The Blue Peace. Rethinking Middle East Water*. Mumbai.

World Bank (2006) *Jordan: An Evaluation of Bank Assistance for Water Development and Management: A Country Assistance Evaluation*. Washington DC.

World Bank (2007) *Making the Most of Scarcity: Accounting for Better Water Management in the Middle East and North Africa*. MENA Development Report. Washington DC: International Bank for Reconstruction and Development.

Chapter 5

Trade and Global Integration in the MENA Region

I. Introduction

Countries in the Middle East and North Africa (MENA) region are home to some of the oldest trade routes in human history, including 1500 years of Silk Road commerce linking Asia and Europe. At the same time however, the region as a whole trades well below its potential and levels of foreign direct investment (FDI) are well below comparators.

Given both static and dynamic gains from trade and the fact that trade has outpaced growth in production over the last 30 years, low levels of trade appear to be a missed opportunity for growth and development.

This chapter explores the MENA region's links with the global economy focusing on trade and FDI. Section I discusses trade and integration performance among MENA countries, and Section II outlines a strategy for boosting the region's global and regional trade and integration.

II. MENA Trade and Integration[1]

- Excluding oil exports, the MENA region with over 400 million people exports about the same amount as Switzerland.
- MENA's share of global non-oil exports has been largely unchanged for 30 years at 2–3% and while it has doubled service exports, it has less than 3% of world total services trade.
- The region's exports remain heavily concentrated in oil and gas; manufactured goods exports account for 11% of total exports (2008–2010).
- However, despite its relatively small share in global trade, openness has been growing, particularly since the 1990s.

  o Trade to GDP ratios rose from less than half to two-thirds of GDP from 1995 to 2008 and MENA's propensity to trade with the outside world rose over and above the world trend for this period.

- Exports more than quadrupled over the period of the late 1990s to the late 2000s from US$194 billion per year to US$825 billion per year while imports grew from US$165 billion per year to US$607 billion per year over the same period.

  o Some 80% of the growth in exports is linked with petroleum.

- Thus, during the 2000s, MENA countries ranked relatively high with respect to global measures of openness and the region is above the world average in terms of exports plus imports relative to GDP.

  o It is generally less open than Asia and Sub-Saharan Africa but above the world average. However, once trade in petroleum and natural resources is excluded, average trade is below the world average.

- A typical MENA country exports 61% below potential to the outside world implying that the region's global exports are about one-third of their potential.

---

[1]This discussion is based on Chaffour (2014), Behar & Freund (2011), Devlin (2010), Owen (1981), and Rouis & Tabor (2013).

- MENA countries also tend to under trade with each other, but the gap is smaller.
  - o Intra-regional exports averaged less than 8% of total exports from 2008 to 2010 relative to 25% in the Association of South East Asian Region (ASEAN) and 66% in the EU. There is also wide variation in the region with Maghreb countries accounting for the lowest share of total intra-regional exports, while Mashreq countries account for the highest share and about three times or more the level of Maghreb intra-regional exports.
  - o However, the importance of regional markets varies by country, accounting for more than half of total non-oil exports in Syria and Yemen for example and between 35% and 40% of non-oil exports in Egypt, Jordan, Kuwait, and Saudi Arabia and about 15% in Jordan.

- In other words, MENA countries tend to trade with each other more than would be expected, conditioning on factors such as size, distance, and others.
  - o On average, the typical MENA country pair under trades with each other by 54% or intra-MENA trade is less than half its potential.

- Nevertheless, the growth benefits of enhanced trade may be limited given that MENA countries have the lowest levels of intra-industry trade or trade in differentiated goods or vertical specialization among developing regions.
  - o On average, intra-industry trade is about 20% of manufacturing in countries such as Egypt and well below 70% shares in East Asian countries.
  - o Component trade is also low, reflecting the low technology content of the region's imports and exports.
  - o This has limited the MENA region's ability to benefit from knowledge spillovers occurring in global production networks.

- The region is also losing market share in traditional export sectors.

○ In 1995, for example, the EU was the dominant market for Maghreb country exports accounting for at least three quarters of total exports.

○ By 2005, however, the EU's share had fallen in every country, while countries such as China have increased shares of the EU market in textiles, apparel, and electronics.

○ Higher imports from China and India have also lowered consumer prices in the MENA region increasing the competition faced by domestic producers particularly in electronics, textiles, leather, and furniture industries.

• Nevertheless, there are some success stories. Since the mid-1990s, manufactured exports as a share of GDP have increased particularly in Jordan, Morocco, and Tunisia and in Jordan and Tunisia, it reached averages of East Asia and the Pacific.

○ However, these exports tend to have relatively low levels of skill and capital intensity.

○ Only Egypt, Jordan, Lebanon, Morocco, and Tunisia are classified as medium or high technology exporters compared to almost 37% of exports in other middle-income countries.

  ▪ Jordan's pharmaceutical industry and Tunisia's electronics industry are two exceptions.

  ▪ Jordan, Morocco, and Tunisia have also acquired more comparative advantage in products closer to the core of world trade such as electronics, machinery, chemicals, road vehicles, and metal manufacturing.

• MENA countries are also host to a growing number of global, regional, and bilateral trade agreements.

○ More than half are members of the World Trade Organization (WTO), most belong to Pan Arab Free Trade Area (PAFTA), and a handful of Mashreq and Maghreb countries have signed Association Agreements with the EU.

○ Turkey has a Customs Union with the EU and has been in negotiations for succession; Bahrain, Jordan, Oman, Morocco have signed Free Trade Areas (FTAs) with the US.

- o Given that the optimal strategy for small countries which cannot influence their terms of trade tends to be unilateral free trade, the proliferation of regional and PTAs poses challenges for future trade policymaking.
- Efforts at regional integration are also on the rise.
  - o In 1957, there was the Arab Economic Unity Agreement, followed by the 1964 initiative by Egypt, Iraq, Jordan, and Syria to form an Arab Common Market.
  - o The Arab Maghreb Union (AMU) was established in 1989 among North African States of Egypt, Tunisia, Morocco, Libya, Algeria, and Mauritania.
  - o In 1997, the PAFTA was initiated, including all 22 Arab League Member states.
  - o In an effort to enhance integration under the Euro-Med-Association Agreements, a handful of MENA countries formed Agadir (Egypt, Jordan, Morocco, and Tunisia) in 2007 which has become one of the more successful efforts at integration.
  - o However, the most successful integration initiative is the Gulf Cooperation Council (GCC) which functions as a Customs Union with free movement of capital and labor.
- Regional diversity in the area of trade policy is high, in terms of measures of openness and tariffs.
  - o Tariffs, for example, are lowest in the GCC and countries as a group tend to be relatively open to global trade.
    - The GCC is negotiating trade agreements with a large number of countries around the world including agreements with European Free Trade Association (EFTA) and Singapore with a forward looking negotiating agenda that includes Australia, China, the EU, India, Japan, Mercosur among others.
- Bilateral agreements are also proliferating.
  - o Jordan has signed bilateral agreements with Bahrain, Egypt, Israel, Morocco, the Palestinian Authority (PA), Sudan, Syria,

and the United Arab Emirates (UAE) and is currently negoti-
ating with the GCC.

- FDI inflows also increased between the 1990s and 2000s particularly after 2002.

  o However, the majority of FDI has been concentrated in three
    countries — Saudi Arabia (23% of total FDI), the UAE (22%
    of FDI), and Egypt (12.3%).
  o Jordan and Morocco each received about 4% of total FDI
    inflows whereas Tunisia and Libya received 3% of the total.
  o This represents a significant shift relative to earlier periods
    when Tunisia, Jordan, and other oil importers received over
    half of all MENA FDI during the 1990s.

- Data analysis suggests a positive link between growth in oil
  prices and growth in MENA FDI over the 2000s as higher
  energy prices significantly raised the attractiveness of FDI in oil
  and gas sectors.

- Overall, inflows remain heavily concentrated in two sectors: real
  estate and mining. Coal, oil, and natural gas and minerals each
  received close to one-third of MENA FDI inflows whereas manufacturing and tourism attracted lower investments. In the GCC
  countries, for example, real estate, mining, and manufacturing
  each attracted about one-fourth of all FDI inflows during the
  2000s while tourism attracted about one-fifth.

- Similarly in Egypt, Jordan, and Libya, the majority of green field
  FDI was directed into real estate and construction sectors while
  in Morocco, the majority went to the mining sector. In Tunisia,
  on the other hand, green field FDI was more distributed across
  sectors.

- Intra-regional investments also increased — GCC countries also
  emerged as important sources of green field FDI in Jordan,
  Egypt, Tunisia, and Libya. Shares of GCC FDI averaged nearly
  60% in Egypt, 70% in Jordan and Tunisia, and 50% in Libya. In
  Morocco, on the other hand, the EU continues to dominate the
  main source of green field FDI. For Jordan, Tunisia and Egypt,
  the UAE and Bahrain are top investors.

- FDI inflows in real estate and mining had limited effects on employment, accounting for an estimated 7% and 5% of FDI related jobs from 2003 to 2011. In contrast, labor intensive food processing, consumer products, and textiles industries accounted for the largest share of FDI related jobs.
- Moreover, the impact of FDI on productivity and technological spillover were highly sector specific.

III. Toward New Directions in Trade and Integration

- Similar to many developing countries, MENA countries were highly globalized during the late 19th century but became more protectionist following the launch of Import Substitution Industrialization (ISI) strategies in the post-independence period.
  - o In the late 19th century, MENA countries were actively engaged in the first period of globalization beginning in the 1870s and continuing until World War I.
  - o Egypt was a one crop exporter and cotton exports were the means for global integration with total trade by 1910–1913 at about 50% of GDP just slightly larger than that of Britain.
    - Moreover, trade with Europe coincided with a fundamental shift in agricultural production towards cash crops and growth in influence of port cities and merchant classes.
    - Countries in the region such as Egypt became widely exposed to the strong expansion of exports of manufactured goods from Europe, particularly from Britain which shifted labor towards agriculture and construction and away from traditional handicrafts such as spinning.
  - o Infrastructure was built up, cities were globalized and trade developed, largely financed by foreign investors. There was some processing of agricultural products, but industrialization was mostly absent.
  - o After World War I, much of the early expansion in trade and commerce gave way to political and economic nationalism as

the gold standard was abandoned and tariffs were imposed on international flows of goods and labor.

- Rapid and large declines in international commodity prices during the Great Depression led to growing protectionism.

o During World War II (WWII), the region was placed under the control of the Anglo-American Middle East Supply Center established in Cairo in 1941 to supply British, French, and later American armies.

- A system of licensing and controls was imposed to restrict trade and conserve shipping space for military supplies.

o By the end of WWII, most countries in the region became newly independent states and trade was subsumed under ISI strategies with high levels of tariffs and quantitative restrictions.

o The collapse of state-led growth models during the late 1970s and 1980s contributed to a shift in trade policies with more emphasis on tariff liberalization, removal of quotas and other quantitative restrictions and export promotion since the 1980s.

- Today, trade policies in the region are formulated by Ministries of trade generally with high involvement by Ministries of Foreign Affairs.

o They contain elements of protectionism as well as liberalization and typically reflect national development priorities along with compliance with multilateral and regional rules and agreements.

- The main challenges facing the region are the need to raise the volume and diversity of exports particularly manufactured exports, raising agricultural and service export potential and improving the competitiveness of trade related infrastructure.
- Manufactured Exports — raising the level of manufactured exports requires simplifying Rules of Origin (ROO) to promote more production integration across the MENA region and better

compliance with technical norms and standards that protect human health, safety, and the environment. There are also issues to be addressed with rising Non-Tariff Measures (NTMs).

o   ROOs are important for building up manufacturing capacity in the MENA region including greater use of supply chains.

o   "Rules of Origin" are the criteria used to define where a product was made.

o   They are an essential part of trade policy in addition to quotas, preferential tariffs, anti-dumping actions, countervailing duties (charged to counter export subsidies), and more.

o   At present, ROOs create a barrier to manufactured export growth and integration among MENA Countries.

  ▪   In Jordan, for example, an estimated 15% of Jordan's manufactured exports from 2000 to 2007 did not use advantageous trade preference rates due to the difficulty of proving adherence to ROOs.

• In particular, MENA country exporters face lengthy procedures for obtaining certificates of origin and difficulty in calculating the raw material value.

o   Existing ROOs are often very restrictive with respect to (i) raw materials that can be used (ii) countries where products can originate from (for instance problems with determining the origins of the fishing vessels for processed fish in Morocco or with textile inputs from Asia as in Tunisia, and (iii) difficulties in complying with the required double transformation rule in textiles — (spinning/weaving or weaving/assembly).

o   Imports from the new EU member states are also not accepted as proof of a product's European origin.

• There is also a need to relax ROOs in terms of country origin, transformation, or value addition.

o   One way to address this is to adopt a regional convention on preferential Pan-Euro-Mediterranean ROOs (with some modification) to replace the network of about 60 bilateral protocols on ROOs in the Pan-Euro-Med zone.

- The Pan-Euro-Med Rules ROOs allow for cumulation of origin for the countries that have an Association Agreement with the EU.
- So inputs originating in one of the countries in the Pan-Euro-Mediterranean can be used in products originating in any other country.
- This makes it easier to integrate production structures.
- However, there would be greater benefits from improving Pan-Euro-Med rules that allow for cumulation and single transformation to qualify for preferential treatment and these could be made more consistent with the rules implied by the agreements with Accession countries.
- This will provide opportunities to integrate production structures among MENA countries as well as facilitate trade among MENA countries with the EU.

- Lack of dynamism in manufactured exports is also linked with lack of competition due to tariffs and protectionism as well as obstacles in the business environment, particularly slow rates of entry and exit in concerned markets.

  o Trade policy barriers are generally divided into tariffs (*ad valorem* and specific) and Non-Tariff Measures (NTMs).
  o While tariffs tend to dominate and are the most widely used policy instrument to restrict trade, their relative importance has been declining.
  o Globally, tariffs have declined significantly linked with WTO negotiation or as a result of PTAs.
  o In 2010–2011, for example, average tariffs imposed by developed countries on all imports were around 5% while average rates on non-agricultural products were 2.5%.

- While a lot of progress has been made in reducing tariffs on goods in MENA countries, more also needs to be done to reduce trade restrictiveness.

  o Trade barriers include all costs of getting a good to the final consumer other than the cost of producing the good itself and includes transportation costs (freight and time) policy barriers (tariffs and non-tariff barriers) and internal trade and transaction costs including domestic information costs, contract enforcement costs, legal and regulatory costs, local distribution, customs clearance, administrative red tape, etc.

- Market access to MENA countries is quite restrictive, particularly for exporters from Latin America and Sub-Saharan Africa.

  o The Overall Trade Restrictiveness Index measures the uniform tariff faced by exporters in all external markets in a manner consistent with the current aggregate export of a country.

  o Based on this measure, the MENA region in particular is restrictive with respect to exporters from Latin America and Sub-Saharan Africa.

- Both unilateral liberalization and PTAs have helped to reduce average tariffs, but there are still challenges.

  o Average uniform equivalents of all tariffs (*ad valorem* and specific) for the region fell from about 14.7% to 6.7% from 2002 to 2007.

  o In addition, despite protectionist pressures following the global financial crisis, tariffs across the region decreased by nearly 1% in 2008–2009, unlike other developing regions.

  o At the level of intra-regional trade, tariffs have declined significantly and have moved to last ranking in terms of most important barriers to intra-regional trade noted by firms over the 2000s.

- However, levels of tariff protection still remain high.

  o According to the Tariff Only Trade Restrictiveness Index, only South Asia has higher levels of tariff restrictiveness in 2008.

    ▪ MENA compares unfavorably with main competitors in Eastern Europe and Central Asia, Latin America, and East Asia, and the Pacific.

  o Empirical evidence suggests sectors such as textiles, chemicals, and food would all benefit from lower effective protection.

- Gravity models using Trade Restrictiveness Indices of the International Monetary Fund (IMF) found coefficients are high and negative for both imports and exports.
- Other studies show that for textiles, chemicals, and food sectors in Egypt, Morocco, and Tunisia, trade liberalization improves export performance.
- Adoption of trade liberalization increases the ratio of sector exports to GDP by around 70% for textiles, 64% for chemicals, and 36% for food.

o Moreover, there are challenges with multiple rates, tariff peaks, and escalating tariffs.

- Most countries in the region have escalating tariff structures.
- In Jordan, for example, in 2008, applied Most Favored Nation (MFN) tariffs showed escalation, negative from the first stage of processing (12.2%) to semi-processed goods (4.4%), and then positive to the final stage of processing (14.4%).
- Escalation is mixed in industries such as textiles and apparel, wood products, and chemicals and plastics but is positively escalated for food and beverages, paper and printing, non-metallic mineral products and basic metal products.
- Reduction of the tariff rates and the number of tariff bands would help to simplify Jordan's tariff structure.

o But this also requires improvements in the business environment particularly with regard to entry.

- Studies suggest that manufactured exports are highly and increasingly specialized in food products, wearing apparel and textiles and that these industries exhibit high mark-ups and low productivity growth.

- Use of NTMs has increased both in terms of the number of products covered and the number of countries using them.

o Also known as behind the border barriers, they include everything from the application of Technical Barriers to Trade (TBTs) to onerous customs procedures.

o   In countries such as Jordan, for example, importers are required to present an importer card for customs clearance purposes or pay a penalty of 2.5% of the value of imports. Individuals, not eligible for the importer card, are charged with the penalty. In addition, an import processing fee of 0.2% (with a minimum of JD10 and a maximum of JD250 per declaration is also collected).

- NTMs such as TBT and sanitary and phytosanitary (SPS) measures, taxes, and subsidies have legitimate public policy objectives such as protecting consumers but can also protect domestic producers from foreign competition.
- NTMs have distributional and productivity implications. When imposed on consumer goods, NTMs can affect poverty and the distribution of income. When imposed on intermediate goods, NTMS affect the competitiveness of domestic firms.
- NTMs are measured in several dimensions including incidence and severity.

o   Incidence is measured by either the frequency ratio (the proportion of product categories covered by one or more NTMs) or the coverage ratio (portion off imports covered) while severity is measured by *ad valorem* equivalents.

o   The *ad valorem* equivalent is the rate of an *ad valorem* tariff that would have had the same effect on imports.

- Over recent decades, NTMs in MENA have shifted from more discretionary instruments such as quantitative restrictions to greater use of technical regulations such as SPS and TBTs.

o   Data on NTMs is limited, but preliminary evidence suggests that in terms of simple measures MENA countries do not stand out in terms of use of NTMs globally.

o   In Egypt, Lebanon, Morocco, Syria, and Tunisia NTMs cover about 40% of products imported by region and 50% of the value of imports.

  - These frequency ratios are roughly similar to other parts of the world and significantly lower than for the EU.

○ However, NTM frequency ratios vary a lot across countries ranging from (15%) in Lebanon to Tunisia (22%), and Morocco (25%), and highest for Egypt at more than 90%.

○ In addition, based on measurements of the types of NTMs used on the same product (more is more restrictive), countries such as Tunisia stand out in terms of using multiple measures relative to Egypt.

○ Empirical studies suggest that countries such as Morocco, Tunisia, and Lebanon have NTMs which penalize out of region imports whereas Egypt and Syria have NTMS which penalize intra-regional imports.

○ When NTMs are included in the calculation of the Overall Trade Restrictiveness Index (OTRI), MENA countries appear quite restrictive.

- The OTRI measures uniform tariff equivalents of the country tariff and non-tariff barriers that would generate the same level of import value for the country in a given year and taking into account the composition of import volume and import demand elasticities of each imported product.

- On the basis of this measure, the MENA region is quite restrictive with some countries such as Egypt, Jordan, and Tunisia more restrictive than Sub-Saharan Africa.

  — This is mainly driven by high NTMs on agricultural goods and manufactures.

  — Transport-related infrastructure and trade-related costs have also become important constraints.

- NTMs in MENA also create gaps between domestic and world prices which are quite large and mainly attributed to SPS measures in Morocco and technical regulations in Tunisia.

  — In Tunisia, the gap ranges from 0% to 105% due to technical regulations and price controls. More generally, while relatively few products are affected by

NTMs for those products which are affected, the price gap is substantial.

- Efforts to address NTMs have largely focused on improving customs and border procedures with some efforts to harmonize product standards.

    o In Jordan, for example, introduction of the Automated Systems for Customs Data (ASYCUDA) is combined with risk based inspection systems.

        ▪ However, a large share of imports is still inspected at the border.

    o Harmonizing industrial standards across countries can be supported with the help of Agreements on Conformity Assessment and Acceptance of Industrial Products and Mutual Recognition Agreements. Such measures can reduce market fragmentation and segmentation created by NTMs particularly for technical regulations.

    o Progress is already underway.

        ▪ The MENA EU Agreement in Morocco, for example, stipulates that all parties shall cooperate in developing the use of Community rules in standardization, metrology, quality control and conformity assessment, including updating of Moroccan laboratories. The aim is to establish mutual recognition agreements for conformity assessment and bodies responsible for intellectual, industrial, and commercial property and for standardization and quality in Morocco.

        ▪ The EC–Tunisia Free Trade Agreement (FTA) has similar language.

        ▪ But the EC–Egypt agreement calls for harmonization on the basis of international standards although by 2008, Egypt had completed harmonization of over 80% of technical regulations with those of the EU.

    o In principle, harmonization with developed country standards can reduce quality uncertainty and improve market access, but adoption of stringent standards as part of a PTA can raise costs for domestic producers and price producers out of other Southern markets where such standards confer no competitive advantage.

- MENA countries also face high levels of NTMs in exporting markets.
  - The EU imposes NTMs on 89% of imports; primarily SPS and technical regulations.
  - Exporters in Tunisia, for example, cite technical regulations, conformity assessment, and SPS measures as being the biggest hurdles by exporters and in the case of agriculture, EU SPS certification costs over US$1,000 per farm.
  - This makes EU SPS certification unaffordable for farmers with less than 100 ha in vegetables and tomatoes or even several hundred acres in citrus production.
- Thus, trade liberalization is still very much on the MENA agenda given the risks of trade diversion and the small economic size of the region.
- Agricultural trade globally remains highly protected and this is also the case for most MENA countries.
  - Tariffs, tariff rate quotas, and non-technical barriers are all used to protect farmers from import competition.
    - On average, developing country exporters face average tariffs of nearly 16% for agriculture and food in developed country markets as compared to less than 10% for textiles and clothing less than 2% for manufactures.
  - The EU in particular poses particular challenges for MENA countries with nearly 2,000 tariff lines for agricultural products.
    - Average tariffs for agricultural products are more than 15% relative to 4% for non-agricultural product and the EU also uses non-*ad valorem* tariffs, tariff rate quotas in which the tariff varies depending on the level of imports,

reference prices (minimum prices at which products can be exported) seasonal restrictions, domestic and export subsidies and NTMs.

- Seasonal tariffs are applied to fresh fruits and vegetables to protect EU growers during the EU growing season.

  o At the same time, Egypt, Morocco, and Tunisia are among the 15 most-protected economies in the world with respect to agricultural production with commodities most protected being wheat, sugar, dairy and livestock products.

- MENA countries would thus benefit from unilaterally reducing import protection for agriculture and gaining better access to EU markets.
- Progress has already commenced. Following the global food crisis, MENA countries unilaterally reduced import tariffs on wheat products and other staples.
- An important aspect of agricultural trade liberalization is food security.

  o The majority of MENA countries are net food importers (with the exception of countries such as Morocco) and most rely heavily on global markets for food staples such as soft wheat.

  o At the same time, domestic agricultural policies encourage farmers to produce basic staples through tariffs and price supports and basic commodities such as bread are heavily subsidized for consumers.

  o Net food imports expressed in caloric terms as a percentage of consumption are over 50% in countries such as Libya, Morocco, and Tunisia and over 25% in Egypt and Jordan and among the highest levels in the world.

  o During the global food crisis of 2007–2008, international prices of wheat, rice, maize, and other commodities were higher and more volatile with an estimated import price increase of 2010 equivalent in cost to 0.6% of total GDP in the region.

- To address this, a number of countries in the region are pursuing policies to promote food self-sufficiency through increases in local staples production.
  - However, this is not likely to mitigate vulnerability to volatile commodity prices.
- Moreover, the opportunity cost of grain self-sufficiency is high.
  - A number of MENA countries export high value agricultural commodities which help generate foreign currency needed to import wheat and wheat flour.
  - Displacing these crops to expand domestic production of wheat and other grain would displace high value crops.
- Thus, greater reliance on trade in cereals (soft wheat) which is relatively low value (relative to fruits and vegetables) and water intensive offers possibilities for importing water resources.
- Global agricultural trade reform is likely to raise world agricultural prices while domestic trade liberalization will reduce domestic agricultural prices relative to world prices.
- MENA countries have comparative advantages in the exports of fruits and vegetables, cotton, olive oil, and other produce.
  - Favorable factors include climate, seasonality and labor costs, relative to European markets.
  - Such advantages could be expanded given better market access, domestic reforms (institutions and regulation) including water management and the ability to comply with SPS standards.
- MENA farmers can indeed compete in markets even if domestic markets are distorted if they have comparative advantages.
  - Egypt, for example, is a competitive exporter of fresh vegetables and rice whereas Morocco exports fresh fruit to Europe and Tunisia is a major exporter of olive oil.

- o Thus, small farmers can compete in the market for fresh fruits and vegetables because their costs of labor are lower relative to the EU and they enjoy a climate more suitable to production of some crops particularly during the European winter.

- MENA countries thus can gain from promoting greater market access in global markets for agricultural commodities they export including fruits and vegetables.

  - o Tunisia in particular would benefit from lower EU tariffs on oil and oil imports, while Egypt would gain from reduced domestic support by the US and the EU for cotton growers.

- However, agriculture has traditionally been excluded from bilateral agreements with the EU.

  - o Nevertheless, empirical studies confirm that the benefits from these agreements would be much larger if liberalization of the agricultural sector was included.
  - o Of particular benefit is lowering EU tariffs and non-tariff barriers on fruits, vegetables, oil, and sugar and simplified regulations for horticultural imports. More technical assistance to comply with SPS regulations regarding meat, fruits, and vegetables and other food imports would also help boost the region's agricultural export performance.

- South–South trade liberalization can also play a role, particularly through regional agreements such as PAFTA and South–South bilateral agreements.

  - o Most of these agreements do not, however, include agriculture and allow many exceptions for sensitive goods, permitting protection to vary by season and granting countries the right to suspend tariff reductions under certain circumstances.

    - Since the costs of protection rise more than proportionately with the level of protection, a small number of exceptions can largely negate the gains from trade liberalization.

- o Thus, there is a need to insist on greater levels of discipline in tariffs and non-tariff barriers applied to agriculture in these agreements.
- o One approach is to reduce the maximum level of tariff protection gradually and contain the highest tariffs first.
  - In Morocco, for example, tariff rates on agricultural imports peak at more than 300% for a number of livestock products.
- Within the region, the modern horticultural sector itself is becoming a key agent of market-oriented reforms.
  - o In Morocco, for example, export farmers are driving private participation in development and management of an irrigation scheme based on public–private partnership investments in a new desalination and irrigation plant.
- In addition, MENA countries could gain significantly from liberalization of domestic agricultural markets.
- Services have become an important sector in global trade in the MENA Region.
  - o However, the MENA region is one of the least open in the world to services trade.
  - o In general, a country cannot become a major services exporter unless it is open to service imports.
    - Opening up trade in services can address supply side constraints and boost competition in the domestic market.
    - Services exports include about 15% of imported services inputs and about a quarter of cross-border services is intra-firm trade.
    - With the fragmentation of production in different stages and development of trade in tasks, services efficiency all along the production chain is a key ingredient of integration.
    - Participation in global production networks depends on a country's ability to efficiently supply onshore and offshore services.

o   In addition, more competitive services can lower trade costs and boost competitiveness.

- Studies estimate that services could represent up to 20% of industrial production costs.
- Commercial services, i.e., transportation, finance are closely linked to trade in goods.

- Egypt, Morocco, and Lebanon are among the top global exporters of commercial services and particularly in Morocco, services exports have expanded rapidly during the 2000s.
- Enhanced liberalization in transport and logistics services in MENA is particularly vital for enhanced services trade as well as manufacturing performance.

o   MENA's geographic proximity to the EU and just-in-time production is a major comparative advantage, but this relies on sophisticated supply chain management.

- Services reform strategies need to be comprehensive and holistic not sector by sector so as to take advantage of bundling opportunities.

o   MENA countries can offer a bundle of tasks with high value added content at key points in global value chains.
o   But this requires more freedom of trade in services and more efficient services provision as well as knowledge transfers.

- At present, there are restrictive regulations among MENA countries in services trade.

o   Measures of service trade restrictiveness include the World Bank Services Trade Restrictiveness Index on policy and regulatory measures affecting international trade in services in 103 countries.
o   Based on this measure, there is considerable protectionism in MENA countries, particularly in the GCC.
o   Most MENA countries in fact are more restrictive than world averages with Egypt and Tunisia being highly restrictive and Morocco less restrictive.

- ○ Protection is also spread across all services which are critical to global value chains including financial, transportation, telecommunications, professional, and retail. These include

  - Barriers to establishment such as strict nationality requirements and movement of persons in professional services which constrain relocation decisions for FDI in some industries.
  - Barriers in retailing and distribution include foreign franchising regulations and pervasive zoning laws which also prevent backward linkages in industry and agriculture when the lead firm is a global retailer.
  - In telecoms in particular, governments limit the number of providers and the extent of foreign ownership.
  - Lack of adequate protection of data in services offshoring.
  - In both banking and insurance, allocation of new licenses is opaque and highly discretionary.
  - In maritime transport, while international shipping is quite open, entry into auxiliary services such as cargo handling is restricted.
  - In air transport, investment in the supply of international and domestic air passenger services is restricted.

- Lack of openness to trade is also reflected in MENA countries commitments to General Agreement on Trade in Services (GATS).

  - ○ These commitments lag behind other developing regions such as Europe and Central Asia.
  - ○ Moreover, MENA offers in the Doha Round negotiation were among the least ambitious and there is reluctance to narrow the gap between Uruguay Round commitments and actual policies.

- Most of the progress in services liberalization has actually occurred through US FTAs concluded with Morocco and Jordan while negotiations with Arab states and the EU are still underway. Bilateral investment treaties and open skies agreements outside the scope of preferential agreements have also helped to liberalize services trade.

- The US–Morocco FTA is the most ambitious agreement in services liberalization in the region. It is based on a negative list approach (top-down, list it or lose it) and Morocco made additional opening efforts compared to its GATS position.
  - It decided not to maintain restrictions on telecoms and open sectors such as ICT enabled services, Business Process Outsourcing (BPO), insurance and postal/courier services.
  - The agreement also includes chapters on liberalization in financial services, telecoms, procurement, investment and e-commerce.
- The US–Jordan FTA is the only US FTA adopting a positive list approach and Jordan did not make significant additional commitments under the FTA.
  - This can be explained in part by Jordan's significantly higher GATS commitments.
- The Euro-Med Process was launched in 1995 with the Barcelona Declaration and boosted in 2004 with the European Neighborhood Policy.
  - Its objective was to create a free trade area through substantial liberalization of trade between the EU and Southern Med Countries (North–South liberalization) and between Southern Med countries themselves (South–South).
  - These agreements cover mostly trade in goods, but services negotiations were opened in 2012 with Egypt, Jordan, Morocco, and Tunisia to establish deeper commitments supplementing GATS with key disciplines in competition, government procurement and investment.
- In the Agadir Agreement (Egypt, Jordan, Tunisia, Morocco), Article 5 relates to trade in services but does not require further liberalization — it respects members' WTO commitments and encourages expansion of trade.
- In the 1989 AMU Agreement (Tunisia, Morocco, Libya, Algeria, Mauritania), Article 2 provides for progressive liberalization of services trade but without details of implementation.

- However, the group has undertaken some shared infra-structure projects related to telecommunications.
  - The 1997 PAFTA does not cover trade in services but a separate framework based on GATS was concluded in 2003.
  - Bilateral agreements between MENA countries do not include services commitments.
  - Bilateral Investment Treaties can also impact services trade and can overlap with commitments in GATS or PTAs (Mode 3).
    - As of 2012, Egypt had concluded 91 such treaties, followed by Jordan 42, Libya 40 and Tunisia 54 (International Center for Settlement of Investment Disputes (ICSID) database).
  - In addition, there are also sector specific agreements in force.
    - In North Africa, for example, both AMU and League of Arab States (LAS) have worked to liberalize air transport; 17 open skies agreements have been concluded among Arab League members and a plurilateral Arab League Open Skies Agreement was concluded in 2004.
    - Morocco also signed an open skies agreement with the EU in 2005 (followed by Tunisia).
  - Of particular importance for future reform of the service sector particularly with regard to Mode 4 is to develop acceptable standards and criteria for licensing and certification of professional service suppliers on the basis of factors such as educational background, qualifying exams, and experience.
  - Progress in liberalization at the sectoral level across MENA countries is progressing in the context of multilateral, regional, and domestic initiatives.
    - In transport and logistics, the role of multilateral liberalization seems limited given its limited coverage under GATS.
    - In maritime and land-based transport, domestic sector reforms are likely sufficient and there is little need for

regulatory harmonization, for example, with the EU or other Arab partners.

— However, there are significant issues with respect to cross-border transport where there are major obstacles to trade.

- In air transport, cross-border liberalization requires changing bilateral air services agreements in addition to national level reforms such as restructuring airlines, privatization of airports and liberalization of ground handling which could be anchored in bilateral or regional agreements.

o In financial services, while these are the second most frequently committed sectors under GATS, the small size of most MENA domestic markets highlights the needs for greater regional integration.

- EU regulations however may not be the most appropriate since they are complex legislation for modern securities markets, while simpler banking and insurance reforms are the top priority for most MENA countries.

o In telecommunications, negotiations have progressed the furthest in multilateral liberalization.

- Domestic reforms should thus be linked with GATS commitments with relatively little value added in terms of regional integration. EU principles and regulations could be useful.

o Electricity is a sector where regional integration could have large benefits through cross-border power transfer for emergency support and peak demand.

- This would allow countries to lower reserve margins which are costly.
- In addition, economies of scale, different load profiles, and complementary energy endowments can potentially enhance gains from trade.
- Private investors would also be more willing to invest in larger markets.

- ○ ICT enabled and business services are one area where more integration with the EU might be beneficial since many EU firms are among world leaders in many business services and there is the potential to benefit from knowledge spillovers and transfers.
  - Most of the liberalization needed however must occur at the national level (unilateral) or through GATS (multilaterally).
  - In some areas such as mutual recognition, more integration might be useful.
- ○ Distribution/retail — there is a strong case for comprehensive liberalization of wholesale distribution given large economies of scale.
  - However, the gap between developed and developing countries' GATS commitments is wide, so there is room for more multilateral liberalization.
  - Opening up distribution to EU retail networks would enhance competition and boost infrastructure investments and spillover.
  - Agriculture and industrial sectors would also benefit.
- ○ Tourism is an area where many reforms have already been undertaken unilaterally given the importance of the sector for foreign exchange earnings. However, there may still be some benefits from deeper South–South integration.
- There are a growing number of success stories in services trade in the region.
  - ○ Morocco, for example, increased shares of services trade in GDP by almost 30% during 2002–2010.
  - ○ However, much of this concentrated in travel and for the region more generally in travel and tourism.
  - ○ Travel alone represents 50% or more of services exports in Egypt, Jordan, and Morocco and close to 50% in Tunisia relative to 25% on average for the rest of the world.

- o In Libya, transport services account for more than 60% of service exports. Shares of financial and communications services are well below world averages.

- Boosting Trade Facilitation:

  - o While MENA's proximity to the 500 million consumers of the EU is one geographic advantage, the flow of goods faces high costs in terms of fees and time.
  - o Trade costs between partners depend in part on geography but also factors such as logistics (price, time, and reliability), customs and other border controls, tariffs, non-tariff barriers and other restrictions to trade.
  - o In the MENA region, GCC countries tend to rank much higher than the rest of the region on measures of logistics and trade related infrastructure.

    - ▪ Free trade zones such as Jebel Ali Free Zone and ports management companies such as Dubai Ports World are some of the best in the world.

  - o Based on measures of Logistics Performance Index (LPI), MENA countries perform better than SSA and South Asia but lag slightly behind East Asia, Latin America and Europe and Central Asia.

    - ▪ The World Bank LPI is based on surveys of logistics professionals who score countries on several dimensions including infrastructure, services, and procedures; the Liner Shipping Connectivity Index of United Nations Conference on Trade and Development (UNCTAD) assesses how well a country is served by container shipping (countries hosting shipping hubs score high) and the cost of trading across borders in the World Bank Doing Business Index is another measure based on firm surveys.

  - o Within the region, it is estimated that a 5% reduction in trade costs between the Maghreb and Western Europe could potentially increase North–South trade by 22% for industrial goods.

- In general, most MENA countries have relatively high levels of "hard" infrastructure port, roads, and airport infrastructure.

  o The problems lie in the area of regulations and procedures and "soft" infrastructure.

  o In addition, much trade activity is geographically concentrated in relatively narrow corridors such as the coastal area in the Mediterranean countries.

  o Within the region, there are relatively few active trade corridors, namely Tunisia–Libya, Turkey–Syria–Jordan and Jordan–Iraq as well as within the GCC.

  o There is no cross-border coordination between countries such as a joint border post and a 2009 World Bank team reported an estimated 10 controls in crossing from Damascus to Amman equally distributed on each side of the border in 2009.

- Morocco has undertaken significant reforms to improve trade-related infrastructure.

  o During 2000s, Morocco undertook significant measures to improve trade related infrastructure by improving logistics and trade connectivity and leveraging its proximity to European markets.

  o The aim was to build capacity for just-in-time exports to Europe, particularly in textiles, electronics, and automotive components.

  o Port capacity was doubled over the last decade by investing in transshipment at Tanger–Med and improved capacity and organization at Casablanca.

  o Port management was also improved by separating landlord functions from operations as well as introducing the participation of the private sector.

  o Connectivity was enhanced through railroad and toll road networks, with plans for continuous transit between Agadir and the Algerian border.

o   Morocco also modernized its logistics policy regime while encouraging private investment in international and domestic logistics services, catalyzing development of new logistics services focused on the manufacturing industry.

o   The government has also promoted development of logistics zones in Casablanca and Tangier.

o   In 2005, measures were introduced to allow warehousing, inventory management, and production under customs oversight.

o   Customs reforms have transitioned more generally toward a risk-management-based approach including the launch of a new customs code in 2011 and the introduction of authorized operators.

References

Behar, A. and C. Freund (2011) The Trade Performance of the Middle East and North Africa. Middle East and North Africa Working Paper No. 53. World Bank.

Chaffour, J. (2014) *From Political to Economic Awakening in the Arab World: The Path of Economic Integration*. Washington DC: World Bank.

Owen, R. (1981) *The Middle East in the World Economy, 1800–1914*. New York: IB Tauris.

Rouis, M. and S. Tabor (2013) *Regional Economic Integration in the Middle East and North Africa: Beyond Trade Reform*. Washington DC: World Bank.

Chapter 6

Industrial Policy for Structural Transformation in the MENA Region

Despite two decades of trade liberalization and reforms, Middle East and North Africa (MENA) countries face challenges in diversifying export products. Non-oil export capacity for this region of 400 million people is comparable to that of Switzerland. Moreover, FDI flows remain concentrated in a handful of sectors and the region is only weakly integrated in global supply chains.

Today, structural transformation and export diversification in particular are becoming vital for raising growth prospects and managing short term vulnerability to external shocks. Without these processes, it will be difficult to address the MENA region's chronic fiscal and trade imbalances and high unemployment. But much of the region's productive capacity is concentrated in a handful of countries, sectors, and firms.

This chapter will discuss the role of industrial policy in promoting export diversification and success in the MENA region. Section I discusses challenges and opportunities for raising export performance among MENA firms, and Section II reviews policies and approaches underway to enhance export performance and diversification.

I. Challenges of Export Diversification in the MENA Region[1]

- MENA countries show limited rates of structural transformation and diversification.

  - Egypt, Morocco, and Tunisia, for example, have experienced sustained growth during the 2000s but did not improve their relative position in the world in terms of per capita income through the 2000s.

    - Moreover, these countries have among the lowest employment rates as a share of the working age population.
    - At the same time, growth in per capita exports has been well below levels in Korea and Thailand despite the fact that during the 1970s, Korea and Thailand started at similar export per capita levels as Egypt and Morocco and well below Tunisia.

- Relative to East Asian Economies, structural transformation appears to have occurred more rapidly in East Asian exporters than MENA countries.

  - Between 1970 and 2008, for example, Egypt transformed itself from a predominantly agricultural and commodity exporter of cotton, rice, and fruits to an exporter of textiles, garments, metal products, and chemicals.
  - Similarly, Morocco's export basket shifted from primary agricultural products and phosphates in 1970 to exports of garments, chemicals, and electronics.
  - Tunisia was an exporter of oil, phosphates, and agricultural products in 1970 but became an exporter of garments, electronics, and chemicals by 2008.
  - China, Korea, and Thailand, on the other hand underwent much more fundamental transformations from export bas-

---

[1]This discussion is based on Lopez-Calix *et al.* (2010), Lederman & Maloney (2012), African Development Bank (2011), Cadot *et al.* (2011), Lederman *et al.* (2009), FIAS (2008) Chaffour (2014), and Schiffbauer *et al.* (2015).

kets dominated by agricultural products and light manufactures to machinery, electronics, and capital intensive goods.

- MENA countries also have high levels of export concentration.
  - o Herfindahl indices for some countries such as Algeria are among the highest in the world (0.42 in 2004).
  - o Moreover, Algeria is ranked among the lowest countries in the world on the basis of rankings such as number of products exported — at 184 compared with 336 in Saudi Arabia, 1,120 in Morocco, 2,489 in Indonesia, and 3,266 in Mexico.
  - o Shares of a single commodity as a percentage of total exports are similarly revealing. Algeria is highly specialized in hydrocarbon exports (98% of export revenues, the highest export concentration of any country in the world (2004).

- Export sophistication is at or below expected levels given per capita income.
  - o Morocco is exporting below what would be predicted given its income level.
  - o Moreover, while Tunisia had a more sophisticated export basket than Korea or Thailand in 1965, it was overtaken by Korea in the 1970s and Thailand in the 1980s.
  - o Diversification has largely occurred through exports of existing products to new markets or on external rather than internal margins.

    - Globally, more than 75% of growth in global manufacturing trade has occurred through growth in intensive margins or more trade in existing categories of goods as opposed to extensive margins or more trade in new products or the disappearance of old products.
    - MENA countries, on the other hand, perform relatively weakly in terms of trade on intensive margins that is increasing or exporting more of existing products to existing markets.

- MENA countries' export baskets are generally in isolated parts of the "product space".

- o The product space is a mapping which measures the distance between two products based on the probability that if a country exports one product, then it exports another.
  - A country that has a comparative advantage in one good is likely to have a comparative advantage in the other.
  - Thus, the distance between any two products is the minimum of the pairwise conditional probabilities of having comparative advantage.

- What about MENA countries? While there is limited analysis of product spaces for MENA countries, there are some tentative findings.
  - o Product space analysis suggests that MENA countries are producing goods competitively in a few products in highly peripheral export sectors such as natural resources and garments and textiles.
  - o Algeria, for example, produces mainly hydrocarbons which are poorly connected to the rest of the product space.
    - Its export basket lies in the sparest part of the product space — it has the least-connected export basket of any country.
    - The implication is that capabilities, necessary for producing hydrocarbons, are difficult to redeploy to other sectors and thus, diversification is difficult.
      - There is almost complete specialization in a very peripheral set of sectors over time, with little movement to new export activities, unlike other oil exporters.
      - Promising export diversification sectors identified for Algeria including those closest to existing exports but up market are agroindustry, steel and alumina, and shipbuilding.
    - Morocco is completely absent from products in the core of the product space since its export products are less complex.

- Tunisia appears in a relatively better position with many nodes in the electronics and sector and some in machinery.
- Egypt has an intermediate position.
- Relative to China, Korea, and Thailand, however, there are significant differences.
- These countries have moved to the dense and more connected parts of the product space.

  — Whereas all developed a presence in garments and textiles, they have moved into more complex activities such as machinery and electronics.

- Limited studies of product quality in MENA countries suggest a number of outcomes.

  o Product quality of MENA exports (expressed in export unit values) is relatively high particularly in comparison with East Asia and the Pacific.

    - Even in categories such as fuel oil, Algeria has one of the highest export unit values, while Yemen and Oman export mid-level qualities.
    - Similarly, in footwear, Morocco, Tunisia, and Israel are on the higher end of product quality.
    - For MENA countries, growth in unit values of exports is relatively low.

      — In general, export unit values of countries further from the quality frontier grow faster than those closer to the frontier (highest observed unit value).
      — MENA countries lag behind East Asia and the Pacific and Latin American Countries (LAC) in measures of quality growth in exports (1990–2001).

- Levels of innovation in MENA exports are also low.

  o While virtually identical goods can be produced at very different levels of sophistication, globally, the capability to produce knowledge intensive and high quality goods appears to concentrate.

- o Mapping countries globally in terms of Revealed Comparative Advantage (RCA) in innovation — that is the total number
  of patents given in particular sector over the total number
  of patents in a country — suggest a number of findings.
    - Very few countries have high comparative advantage in both
      exports and innovation across products.
    - Most MENA countries are lacking in RCA for exports
      and/or innovation while countries such as Korea, Japan
      have high RCA in both dimensions. Israel comes the
      closest.

- High export volume is also linked with more specialization.

  - o For most countries including in the MENA region, manu-
    facturing exports are dominated by a few "big hits" which
    account for most of the export value and where the hit
    includes finding the right product and the right market.
  - o For example, in a study of export "big hits" out of 2,985 pos-
    sible manufacturing products and 217 destinations, Egypt
    gets 23% of its total manufacturing exports from exporting
    one product — ceramic bathroom kitchen items to one desti-
    nation, Italy, capturing 94% of the Italian import market for
    that product.

- Large export "superstars" tend to dominate.

  - o Globally, while most firms export a small number of prod-
    ucts, most exports are done by a handful of firms shipping
    many products.
  - o These large, global multiproduct firms exporting to multiple
    locations thus play a dominant role in global trade.
  - o Superstar exporters are a driving factor behind RCA, the
    top 1% of exporters contribute over three quarters of export
    growth across countries.
    - In the MENA region, export superstars generate about
      half of total exports and the average number of export
      superstars per country is over 40.

— However, numbers of superstars vary widely within the region, from 5 in Yemen to almost 80 in Egypt.
— Where do superstars in MENA originate? Empirical evidence suggests that superstars tend to start as large firms (operating 10 years ago) or new firms entering the market.

⇒ Superstars also have significant staying power — in Morocco, for example, over 80% of past superstars remained in the top 5% in recent years.

— Among the new "superstar" market entrants in MENA, growth was rapid.

⇒ In 2010, for example, it took new firms only 1.5 years to reach superstar status in Morocco.
⇒ Moreover, MENA superstars are active across a wide range of sectors from machinery, metals, and apparel to plastics, wood, chemicals, textiles, and foodstuffs.
⇒ The overwhelming majority of firms are either producers or manufacturers, not traders, as is the case in Jordan.
⇒ The majority of superstars also tend to be foreign owned. In Jordan, for example, more than half of export superstars are linked with foreign capital.

II. Raising Export Success in the MENA Region — What Can be Done?

• Industrial policies in the MENA Region:

o The MENA region has a long history of using industrial policy to promote industrial development but has only recently applied such more "active" approaches to export diversification.
o Common policy measures have included high levels of state intervention and investment in strategic industries with the

purpose of building a domestic industrial base. Subsidies and tax breaks also played an important role.

- In Egypt, for example, industrial policy measures have been adopted since the early 1950s under the umbrella of state-led import substitution industrialization.

  — Beginning in the 1950s through the 1970s, policies included state investment in heavy industry, favorable tax treatment for some private investments and a generally heavily regulated private sector.
  — By the 1970s, the failure of such approaches was becoming evident and policies shifted towards encouraging private investment in favored sectors.
  — However, price regulations, customs, and financial sector policies all continued to support state-owned enterprises while devaluation and limited de-regulation together with tax breaks gave some boost to private investment.
  — From the mid-1980s to the 1990s, private investment increased alongside growing business interests of the army into construction, tourism, white goods, vehicles fertilizers, and others.
  — The 1990 fiscal crisis contributed to a shift in policy with important privileges for favored sectors and firms retained together with tax holidays, efforts to liberalize the financial sector, and reduce barriers to trade and international capital flows. Commodity prices were also deregulated.
  — From 2004 to 2011, policy shifts were more dramatic. The government privatized 87 state-owned enterprises in 2004–2005, lowered income taxes and simplified customs procedures and start-up regulations. Liberalization of the financial sector also continued. In addition, there was a shift in policy focus to new markets (subsidies to exports) combined with new production technologies (subsidies for modernization).

— Nevertheless, large parts of the economy continued to remain closed to foreign investors particularly aviation and engineering services, heavy industry in the form of energy production, steel and aluminum production, construction, insurance, and fertilizer.
— Clientelism was also on the rise. After 2000, 17% of ruling party deputies and five ministers were actively engaged in businesses relative to 8% prior to 2000.
— Egypt's Industrial Development Policy was a flagship effort at addressing failures in training (Industrial Training Council), promoting quality assurance (National Quality Council), innovation and technology transfer (Technology and Innovation Centers) and finance (Industrial Modernization Center) together with addressing imperfect information about market opportunities (Export Council and Export Development Bank). It similarly addressed problems of coordination in infrastructure and plant location (Industrial Development Agency).
— However, in practice, implementation of the strategy was non-transparent and favored some groups over others. It is estimated that beneficiary firms received export subsidies of up to 15% of the value of goods and up to 95% of modernization costs, large enough to offset public policy distortions in finance, human capital, and administrative interference but also large enough to confer significant rents.
— There was generally little transparency around targeting of benefits to insider firms.
— Moreover, while FDI during this period grew rapidly, it remained relatively concentrated in real estate and mining as opposed to tradable manufacturing sectors, limiting the potential spillovers for economic development and structural transformation.
— Few market failures in the form of limited research and development and insufficient coordination of complementary activities were effectively addressed.

— Thus, structural transformation did not fully materialize in Egypt in terms of product variety increases and TFP growth.

— From 1980 to 1999, for example, product concentration actually increased as variety fell and industrial sectors which received the most assistance generally exhibited the lowest rates of productivity growth.

— Unlike East Asian economies, Egypt's industrial policies did not target new activities, did not make assistance to firms performance based, such as, on export success and did not include sunset clauses for supported sectors and firms.

— Moreover, in some cases where reforms had the potential to enhance market competition such as tariff reductions, they were frequently counterbalanced by increases in other protective measures such as non-tariff measures (NTMs).

⇒ While average tariffs fell by nearly half from 16.5% in 1995 to 8.7% in 2009, NTMs increased. In 2009, for example, of the 53 different NTMs in place, almost half were introduced or amended around 2000 and 21% between 2005 and 2009.

o In Morocco, on the other hand, industrial policy has shifted between providing selectively targeted benefits and benefits to all exporters.

■ During the 1980s, for example, efforts focused on boosting manufacturing industries with the help of tariffs and licenses. At the same time, however, the real exchange rate depreciated by 40% providing a substantial boost to exports and manufacturing.

■ During the 1990s, the government adopted trade liberalization measures including reducing tariffs and other licensing requirements while lessening direct credits for exporters and allowing greater market forces in the allocation of credit.

■ However, manufacturing and the economy at large were generally stagnating, likely affected to some extent by the 22% appreciation of the real exchange rate.

■ By the 2000s the government began to use selective investment promotion measures to boost exports, jobs, and structural transformation.

— The Hassan II Fund for Economic and Social Development was created providing investment subsidies in the amount of about US$560 million primarily for textile manufacturing and automotive suppliers.

— At the same time, other policy instruments were modified to support a comprehensive industrial policy program, Plan Emergence which aimed to modernize the industrial sector and offshoring.

— Agro Food, seafood, textiles, automotive, aeronautics, electronics, and offshoring services in French and Spanish were targeted.

— Foreign investors as well as domestic firms gained access to investment incentives. In general, however, market failures were not defined and the effects of subsidies not evaluated.

— Implementation of the policy was influenced by business groups such as Confederation General des Entreprise du Maroc (CGEM) which at first attempted to forestall tariff reductions but rescinded when the government responded by including more small and medium sized firms in the CGEM. An anti-corruption campaign launched by the government also targeted some businesses while at the same time, the government included more business representatives into the legislature.

— Overall, such policy measures and actions did not have a significant effect on structural transformation and export diversification.

— In part, the level of financial transfers was small, particularly in comparison with East Asia's industrial policy. In 2010, incentives amounted to approximately 0.7% of GDP or US$612 million.

o In Syria, manufactured exports became the target of the 10th Five Year Development Plan (2006–2010) and initiatives included investment and export promotion agencies (EPA) and industrial cities.

  ▪ Support from international donors in the form of the Industrial Modernization and Upgrading program included support to textile and clothing sectors although the program did not respond to explicit market failures nor was there an evaluation of the impact of subsidies.

o Initiatives in Jordan have largely focused on support to small and medium enterprises, creation of the Jordan Investment Board charged with improving the business environment including tax incentives to investors and the development of four regional zones targeting specific industries.

  ▪ Less transparent measures have included tax incentives granted to selected firms and industries by the Council of Ministers with little transparency with respect to conditions and evaluation procedures.

o The Gulf Cooperation Council (GCC) states have adopted a slightly different approach.

  ▪ The major thrust of industrial policy has been targeted to development of the energy sector.
  ▪ During the 1970s, for example, Saudi Arabia began to develop its own technical capacity in oil production through construction of facilities for oil refining and petrochemicals.
  ▪ Industrial cities in Jubail and Yanbu were created and governed by a Royal Commission in 1975 which operates outside of the ministry structure and has complete autonomy over spatial planning, regulation and investments in the cities.

- The goal was to create a cluster of subindustries related to petroleum products and petrochemicals including related logistics capabilities. Production in the cities is owned by Saudi Aramco and Sabic, a government created petrochemical company or joint ventures (JVs) with these companies and international partners.
- As a result, Saudi Arabia has created industrial capacity based on oil and gas inputs supplied below export prices.
- Dubai on the other hand built industrial and service clusters around the Jebel Ali Free Zone and vast investments in transport infrastructure. It has also encouraged foreign investment in finance and real estate.

- As surveyed earlier, most MENA countries have attempted to boost structural transformation and export diversification with the help of a number of programs and policy measures.

  o Primary among these are export promotion and free trade zones and industrial clusters.

- Export promotion:

  o Export promotion programs include support for export product development and upgrading, export credit, and insurance to lower upfront costs of export market entry and marketing support.
  o In the MENA Region, the *Fonds d'Accès aux Marchés d'Exportation* (FAMEX II) program is one of the most successful and provides assistance to new exporters through matching grants.
  o The program was launched in 2005 and has supported more than 1,000 firms on a cost-sharing basis through matching grants covering 50% of investment expenditures.

    - An impact evaluation based on 2004–2008 data suggests that FAMEX II improved Tunisia's export potential, particularly among new exporters.
    - According to the evaluation, most FAMEX II applicants were relatively large and minimum thresholds for grant

eligibility were set at US$140,000 (manufacturing) and US$70,000 (service) in sales.

- Eligibility for receiving a FAMEX II grant required that firms submit export development plans and specify whether these activities developed new products, new markets and/or skills in the case of first-time exporters.

  — Of the 2,000 eligible manufacturing firms already exporting in 2004, 20% applied for FAMEX II funding and more than 70% of applicants were accepted into the program.

- Grants were then distributed on the basis of a review of export development plans by a committee of senior exporters from the management team and detailed interviews with firm applicants.

  — In some cases, FAMEX II also helped firms revise their export plans and facilitated technical assistance and training during implementation.

- Eligible activities included support for entering new export markets such as market research, training, and consulting.

  — Matching funds were required by applicants, requiring firms to use their own resources in export development efforts. This was intended to produce a better and more homogenous group of applicants relative to full grants.

- Results of an impact evaluation of the program are promising.

  — From 2004 to 2008, the average annual growth rate of export values was nearly 40% higher for FAMEX II participants relative to the control group.

  — Moreover, FAMEX II had a measurable impact on export diversification potential (new products, new markets): average annual growth was 5% higher in the number of exported products and 4.5% higher for export destination countries.

— The program particularly helped first-time exporters, that is, firms that started exporting for the first time with FAMEX II assistance.

o Two design features were considered particularly important for the project's impact and potential success:

- Matching grants and cost sharing as opposed to non-financial support (i.e., consulting, funding for travel).
- The size FAMEX II grants was relatively large with FAMEX II spending more per participant than similar programs elsewhere with the size of grants averaging US$70,000.

- Expert Promotion Agencies (EPA):

o Well functioning, focused and generally smaller EPAs can raise export and trade potential through image building, export training, marketing support, and research.

- Global evidence suggests that on average US$1 of export promotion assistance is linked with a US$300 increase in exports.

o Limited evidence suggests however that EPAs among MENA countries are generally less effective relative to other developing regions.

- Assistance is more effective when it incorporates a high level of private sector participation, is focused on non-traditional exports and larger firms and bundles its assistance — that is, product development and marketing together with export financing.

- Clusters and Free Trade Zones:

o In recent years, cluster development has also become an important instrument for trade, investment, and industrial policy to stimulate growth and global integration.

- Clusters are interconnected systems of companies, suppliers, service providers, and associated institutions linked by externalities and complementarities. They are based on forces of agglomeration.

- Clusters in the MENA Region — What do we know?
  - Clusters and Special Economic Zones (SEZs) were established as early as the 1960s and 1970s in Egypt, Jordan, and Syria.
  - Most SEZs can be characterized as free zones and seek to attract FDI through tax incentives and high-quality infrastructure.
    - Limited evidence suggests some impact — SEZs are estimated to have generated 8% of employment in Tunisia and 25% in the United Arab Emirates in recent years.
  - Approaches to SEZs differ across the region:
    - GCC countries, such as the United Arab Emirates have leveraged the global success of the Jebel Ali Free Zone to house more than 30 economic zones covering a wide range of sectors, including industry, information technology research and development, media, and entertainment.
    - In Jordan and Egypt, SEZs are more limited in focus.
  - Principle challenges with SEZs in the MENA region include:
    - Strict boundaries between SEZ activity and the local business environment have created a "dual" economy with limited interaction and spillover. This has been the case with the offshoring sector in Tunisia, for example.
    - SEZs also rely heavily on regulatory incentives — cutting red tape and simplifying administrative procedures for firms in the zones.
    - One of the main benefits of SEZ activity in the GCC countries is exemption from foreign ownership and labor market restrictions.

o   Dubai's Construction Services Cluster:

- This cluster represents a significant (disproportionately large) share of the economy nearly one-fourth GDP. Growth from 2001 to 2007 was 12% in real terms. Moreover, its size is also large as share of fixed capital formation.

- Three main segments of the cluster include infrastructure, commercial properties, and residential. The first two require large projects and are international in focus; the residential segment however is based more on local competition.

- Studies suggest that this cluster is relatively deep compared to other countries but heavily skewed towards real estate development (2/3 total projects). In addition to real estate developers and construction companies, specialized suppliers and service providers which have emerged, each with a wide range of specialized service providers supply inputs to core players. These include financial services, tourism, transport, and logistics related clusters which provide specialized services and contribute to demand for the construction cluster. There are also dedicated government agencies, industry associations, and educational institutions.

- The history of construction services in Dubai dates to the 1930s. One of the first companies created provided services to British forces in the region. Until the 1970s, the sector remained small and focused on limited local demand.

- However, rising oil revenues and ambitious infrastructure development such as the construction of Jebel Ali and other zones boosted the growth of the clusters dramatically.

- Initially, international construction companies were the only companies with sufficient expertise to undertake such large projects and entered the market on a large scale. Many of the local companies formed as JV partners with foreign companies.

- With the collapse of oil prices in the 1980s, international companies generally left the region and local companies remained and served a smaller local market with few exports.
- By the late 1990s, a new phase of the cluster emerged with the creation of large real estate developers by the government, namely Emaar and Nakheel.
- Growth was catalyzed by development of residential complexes allowing *de facto* property ownership in Dubai for other GCC nationals and foreigners investors attracted by an open business environment. Thus, local and expatriate demand drove demand for residential construction.
- Between 2001 and 2008 foreign investment is estimated to have been US$30 billion and the Government of Dubai also began to invest heavily in tourism and infrastructure creating large demand for hotel capacity.
- This contributed to significant growth in domestic and foreign companies serving the market and strained domestic capacity. Prices soared and the government began to set maximum prices for key supplies such as cement and exempting cement and steel imports from customs duties.
- After the 2008 financial crisis, the cluster collapsed under the weight of high debt on balance sheets of real estate developers. This was compounded by a decline in real estate prices, effectively launching a new phase of cluster rationalization and realignment to focus on building capabilities as opposed to land development.
- Going forward, the ability to rescale and downsize successfully will depend on the cluster's capacity to build unique capabilities of firms. In the past, however, construction companies were generally lacking knowledge intensity and skills.

References

African Development Bank (2011) *Comparative Study on Export Policies in Egypt, Morocco, Tunisia and South Korea*. Mandaluyong.

Cadot, O., A Fernandes, J. Gourdon, and A. Mattoo (2011) *Where To Spend the Next Million? Applying Impact Evaluation to Trade Assistance*. Washington DC: World Bank.

Chaffour, J. (2014) *From Political to Economic Awakening in the Arab World: The Path of Economic Integration*. Washington DC: World Bank.

Foreign Investment Advisory Service (2008) *Special Economic Zones: Performance, Lessons Learned, and Implications for Development*. Washington DC: World Bank.

Ketels, C. (2009) *Clusters and Dubai's Competitiveness*. Dubai Economic Council, Dubai, October 2009.

Lederman, D., M. Olarreaga, and L. Payton (2009) Export Promotion Agencies Revisited. World Bank Policy Research Working Paper No. 5125. Washington DC: World Bank.

Lopez-Calix, J., P. Walkenhurst, and N. Diop (eds.) (2010) *Trade competitiveness in the Middle East and North Africa: Policies for Export Diversification*. Washington DC: World Bank.

Maloney W. and D. Lederman (2012) *Does What You Export Matter? In Search Of Empirical Guidance for Industrial Policies*. Washington DC: World Bank.

Schiffbauer, M. *et al.* (2015) *Jobs or Privileges: Unleashing the Employment Potential of the Middle East and North Africa*. Washington DC: World Bank.

Chapter 7

The Challenge of Private Sector Development in the MENA Region

Relative to other developing regions, most Middle East and North Africa (MENA) countries have relatively low levels of private investment and private sector activity. Moreover, the business landscape is populated by a handful of globally successful firms and large growing numbers of low productivity very small and medium-sized firms (SMEs). Market dynamism is hampered by low business entry and firm growth is constrained by market-segmentation regulations and enforcement. Underdeveloped financial markets also play a role.

This chapter explores private sector activity in the MENA region from a number of perspectives including private investment, business environment, and the dynamics of firm entry and exit. Section I discusses private investment in the MENA region; Section II discusses firm dynamics and the business environment, and Section III concludes with policy measures to boost private sector activity including the role of financial markets.

I. Private Investment in the MENA Region[1]

- In the MENA region, private investment has maintained relatively lower shares of GDP compared to other developing regions and relative to public investment.
- Average investment rates for MENA, for example, were 25% from 1974 to 2007, a rate higher than all other developing regions with the exception of East Asia and the Pacific (30%) and outpacing high income countries.[2]
- However, shares of private investment as a percentage of GDP remain considerably smaller, averaging 15% for 1987–2007.[3]

  o Relative to the 1980s and 1990s, however, this trend has shifted slightly with shares of private investment in GDP rising from an average of 13% and 15% in the 1980s and 1990s respectively to 17% during the 2000s.

II. The MENA Private Sector — What do We Know?

- Relative to industrialized countries, developing countries tend to have much larger numbers of smaller firms and wide gaps in productivity across firms, many times within the same industry.

  o A large portion of small producers also operate outside government regulation and rely heavily on informal credit

---

[1] This discussion is based on Beck *et al.* (2005), Rocha *et al.* (2011), Sekkat (2010), World Bank (2009), Rijkers *et al.* (2014), Chaffour (2014), Schneider *et al.* (2010), Schiftbauer *et al.* (2015), Ayyagari *et al.* (2011), Stone & Badawy (2011), Elbadawi & Loayza (2008).

[2] Average is based on World Development Indicators (WDI) data on Gross Capital Formation as a Share of GDP for the following countries: Algeria, Egypt, Iran, Israel, Jordan, Kuwait, Morocco, Oman, Saudi Arabia, Syria, Tunisia, and Turkey for which data is available.

[3] Average is based on limited data availability for WDI Gross Fixed Capital Formation Private Sector as Share of GDP for Algeria, Egypt, Iran, Jordan, Morocco, Syria, Tunisia, and Turkey.

markets and internal funds for finance. They are relatively labor intensive and account for a larger share of employment than output.

- In the MENA region, most private firms are classified as Micro and SME.

  o Micro and SMEs, accounting for a dominant share of private non-agricultural activity-estimated at 97% of firms in Egypt.
  o In Turkey, on the other hand, this sector accounts for about 27% of value added.
  o Nearly half of all employees in the manufacturing sector in Jordan, for example, are employed by firms with less than 20 employees and these firms represented more than 90% of all manufacturing establishments.
  o More recent evidence for Tunisia suggests that firm size distributions are becoming more skewed towards smaller firms.

    - From 1996 to 2010, for example, one person firms accounted for 83% of all firms and 28% of employment.
    - On average, there were only 51 firms that employed more than 1,000 employees.

- A dualistic firm structure and wide productivity gaps:

  o Industrial structures tend to be characterized by a large number of small, inefficient firms and a handful of large and in some cases highly successful global firms.
  o Aramex, a global logistics supply company founded in Jordan, was the first Arab company listed on the US Nasdaq exchange and is active in 33 countries.
  o On average, value added per worker of a firm near the top of the distribution (80th percentile) is almost seven times higher than average firms near the bottom, relative to 2.4 times in Malaysia.
  o Productivity in Turkey's construction sector is more than twice the level of productivity in agriculture and productivity in manufactures is almost three times as large.

- o Moreover, in Turkey on average, the modern segment of firms is almost three times more productive than the traditional segment.

- There is weak dynamism in the MENA private sector as suggested by relatively low entry and exit rates and limited mobility.

  - o MENA countries have relatively low rates of firm entry and exit.
  - o Measures of entry density or the number of newly registered firms per 1,000 people ages 15–64, are well below comparators.

    - In 2012, for example, data were available for 80 countries and only 26 of those had an entry density below that of Jordan.
    - Croatia's working age population is comparable in size to Jordan's, but the average number of newly registered firms in Croatia was almost five times higher in 2004–2009.

  - o Overall, gross entry and exit rates in countries such as Columbia are 11% and 12% higher.
  - o Firm survival rates differ within the region and are higher in Tunisia than in West Bank and Gaza, Jordan, and Turkey.

    - In Turkey, about 60% of firms with more than 20 employees in 2006 are projected to have fallen to fewer than 20 employees in 2011.

  - o On average, MENA firms tend to be relatively older than firms in other developing countries.

    - The median age of a local manufacturing firm is nearly 20 years relative to 10 in Eastern Europe and Central Asia and East Asia and the Pacific.
    - Firm surveys suggest declining rates of mobility and growth.

- In Morocco, for example, surveys of manufacturing firms (1985–2003) suggest:

  - o Average annual entry rates were 9.1% whereas, exit rates are lower at 5.2% and below other developing countries.

- ○ Firm entry and exit rates also tended to move in the same direction through time, with rates decreasing until 1994 and then showing an upward trend.
- ○ Entering firms were small:
  - New entrants accounted for about 3% of each sector's output and produced about 24% of the level of output of incumbent firms.
  - About 5% of firms exited each year and exiting firms had a small market share (about 1% on average).
  - The impact of new entrants on employment was similarly moderate because most new entrants are small.

- Newer studies suggest limited mobility.
  - ○ In Tunisia, for example, between 1996 and 2010 most firms in the sample did not grow, even in the long run and very few firms changed size class.
    - The self-employed were least likely to expand into a larger size class.
    - Only 2% of firms employing between 10 and 50 people in 1996 employed more than 100 workers by 2010.
    - Between 1996 and 2010 for example, most firms in the sample did not grow even in the long run and very few firms changed size class.
  - ○ Moreover, the probability that medium-sized firms grow to become large four years later is low.
    - For firms with 20–49 employees, it is 13.5% in Turkey, 11.9% in Egypt and Morocco, 10.7% in the West Bank and Gaza, and 9.8% in Jordan.

- Economic activity remains concentrated, particularly in the industrial sector.
  - ○ In Jordan, for example, more than 50% of value added is concentrated in a few industries which vary in terms of the importance of entry and sunk costs including textiles and wearing apparel, food products, and chemicals.

   o In Morocco, manufacturing is concentrated in clothing, leather and shoes, chemical products, textiles and other food products.

      ■ During the 1980s and 1990s, half of sales in six sectors were accounted for by four or fewer firms.

      ■ There is a statistically significant positive correlation between shares of public ownership and industrial concentration.

      ■ Moreover, industry price-cost margins are linked with concentration factors.

• Many MENA firms tend to be single product firms.

   o Firm surveys in Morocco during the 1980s, for example, suggest that the overwhelming majority of firms are single product firms with 50% to 92% of respondent firms manufacturing only one product.

      ■ In only four sectors did 10% or more of firms produce three products or more and three of these sectors were exports (textiles, clothing, and chemical products).

      ■ Firms with high shares of exports were more diversified and also more productive. Much of this depends on individual sectors and industries. Moreover, younger firms are less diversified.

• Privileges granted to politically connected firms create barriers to entry, profitability, and disincentives to compete in global markets.

   o In Egypt, 45% of all connected firms operate in energy intensive industries relative to 8% of all firms and energy subsidies benefit a handful of politically connected firms.

   o In Tunisia, 64% of politically connected firms are in sectors requiring an exclusive license to operate relative to 45% of non-connected firms.

      ■ Moreover, cumbersome business regulations, including barriers to entry and trade protect a few firms.

- o Firms in politically connected industries are 11–14% more likely to have acquired land from the government.
- SMEs in the MENA region are a growing focus among policy makers because of their potential impact on employment.
  - o Global studies of employment among developing countries including for MENA countries (Yemen, Turkey, Israel) during the 2000s suggest that firms with 5–250 workers and more than 11 years old employ more than 60% of total, permanent full time employment.
    - However, the importance of SME contribution to employment is negatively linked with per capita income.
      - In middle income and upper middle income countries, for example, larger firms with more than 500 employees have the second highest employment shares (23% in lower middle to 28% in upper middle).
  - o Other studies suggest some variation across countries.
    - In Egypt and the West Bank and Gaza, for example, the majority of employment occurs in very small firms (60%) relative to Jordan (40%) Tunisia (37%).
    - Overall, shares of jobs in firms with at least 1,000 employees are less than 10%.
- Young, large firms in developing countries including the MENA region are important for dynamism and innovation.
  - o Recent studies have focused on a group of fast-growing young firms which generate high sales and employment.
    - In Egypt, these firms, labeled "gazelles", are SMEs that grew an average of 20% or more over more than 4 years.
      - They are active in both manufacturing and service sectors.
    - Factors contributing to high growth include training employees, using email or having a company website,

being less than 10 years old, getting a high number of inspections, experiencing fewer power interruptions, and using foreign-licensed technology.

- Moreover, in Lebanon and Egypt, gazelles are found to be more productive than non-gazelles.
- In Tunisia, the majority are located in textiles, construction, and real estate, while in Jordan they are concentrated in the construction sectors.

o More generally, young startups are generating a large proportion of new jobs in MENA.

- In Tunisia, micro-startups generated 580,000 new jobs between 1996 and 2010 accounting for 92% of all net job creation.
- In Lebanon, micro-startups generated about 66,000 jobs between 2005 and 2010 accounting for 177% of net job creation.
- The second largest number of jobs was created by young large firms with 2,000–2,999 employees.

o This is similar in some ways to developed countries such as the US where startups are important for employment but also where young firms are subject to more mobility and an "up and out" dynamic.

- In the US, for example, startups create about 3% of employment but 20% of job creation.

- Limited evidence suggests that the informal economy in the MENA region may not be disproportionately large, given per capita income levels.

o The shadow or informal economy is characterized by economic activities and income derived from them that circumvent or otherwise avoid government regulation, taxation, or observation.

o A more specific definition includes all market-based legal production of goods and services that are deliberately concealed from public authorities for any of the following reasons.

- This includes avoiding payment of income, value added or other taxes, avoiding payment of social security contributions, avoiding certain legal labor market standards such as minimum wages, maximum working hours, safety standards, etc. and avoiding complying with certain administrative questionnaires or other administrative forms.

- A recent global study of shadow economies suggests that such activities account for nearly one-fifth of GDP in over 160 countries between 1999 and 2006/2007.
- Driving forces of the shadow economy include increased burdens of taxation, labor market regulations, the quality of public goods and services and the state of the "official" economy.

  o The degree of intensity in enforcement of these regulations is a key factor.

- On a global scale, limited studies suggest that MENA countries tend to have relatively small informal production sectors.

  o Bahrain, Saudi Arabia, Iran, Oman, Jordan, Syria, and Jordan, for example, were ranked among the top tier of countries with the smallest shadow economies (i.e., less than 20%).

  o Countries in the middle of the global distribution include Morocco, Tunisia, and Lebanon with more than 30% of GDP accounted for by the informal economy.

  o No MENA countries in the sample were included in the "high" category of 50% or more.

  o Shadow economies tend to be smaller in GCC countries.

- Other studies of informal labor markets suggest slightly different results.

  o Measures of informality for MENA countries tend to be higher than predicted on the basis of various indicators.

III. Raising Private Sector Activity for Employment and Growth in the MENA Region

- Higher private sector activity has the potential to benefit MENA countries in two important ways: boosting employment and productive potential.
- To this end, a large number of MENA countries are implementing policies to promote the growth of SMEs.
  - In general, such policies are justified on the basis that SMEs are (i) engines of innovation and growth; (ii) important for poverty reduction because of labor intensive and job growth; and (iii) constrained by market and institutional failures.
  - In practice, however, large exporting firms are typically the primary mechanism through which technologies are adapted to local circumstances and boost productivity growth and there is mixed evidence regarding the role of SMEs in job creation.
    - In general, large firms tend to provide more stable, higher quality jobs than small firms.
  - Cross-country evidence further explores the role of SMEs in economic growth, poverty alleviation, and income inequality and finds a strong positive association between the size of the SME sector and the rate of economic growth, but not that SMEs in fact cause growth.
- Thus, promoting SMEs at the expense of other firms may be counterproductive, particularly in the MENA region where small firms tend to suffer from lack of dynamism and mobility.
- From a growth perspective, the important issue is not the size of the SME sector per se but its dynamism, that is, the extent to which there is entry of new firms and the possibilities for successful SMEs to grow.
  - This process includes introduction of new products and new technologies as well as signing joint ventures with foreign partners or obtaining new licensing agreements. Other actions that can potentially expand the size and profitability

of firms include opening a new plant or outsourcing a productive activity.

- Access to finance is particularly important for growth by improving the allocation of resources and investment.
  - Financial markets also affect the distribution of economic opportunity.
    - By channeling resources to individuals on the basis of individual skill and initiative rather than family wealth or social status, the financial system influences economic opportunities.
    - More specifically, financial markets help to influence who can launch a business venture and who can live in areas that foster good schooling for children.
  - For firms in the MENA region, access to finance is a primary constraint to growth.
    - An estimated 20% of SMEs have a loan or line of credit, lower than any other region and only 10% of investment expenditures are financed by bank credit.
    - While MENA banks regard the SME segment as potentially profitable and most banks are engaged in SME lending, relationship-based lending tends to prevail and suggests that financial infrastructure remains deficient.
    - Shares of SME lending are 8% on average for the region; 2% in the Gulf Cooperation Council (GCC) and 13% in non-GCC countries.
      - These targets are generally well below banks' own long run targets which suggest further lending potential to SMEs.
  - In general, raising access to finance for SMEs requires improving efficiency and scope in financial instruments.
    - Given that fixed costs such as credit assessment, processing, and monitoring make it costlier to lend to SMEs there is a need to lower the costs of small-scale lending.

- Empirical evidence suggests that transaction-based lending approaches can be more cost effective, particularly if carried out by large financial institutions that can exploit economies of scale.
- Foreign banks are more likely than domestic banks to use transaction based lending techniques and more centralized business models and do not necessarily lend less to SMEs relative to other banks.

  — Thus, there is clearly a role for large and foreign firms in SME financing given that they may have a comparative advantage through arms-length lending technologies to SMEs such as asset-based lending, factoring, leasing and fixed-asset lending, credit scoring, and centralized organizational structures.

- Moreover, leasing or lending based on the cash flow of the financed asset such as machinery is a particularly attractive financing tool for SMEs given that it is based on a financed asset rather than the reputation or asset base of the company and frequently includes tax advantages and easier recovery with the right legal framework.
- Similarly, factoring or the discounting of accounts receivables is another useful lending instrument for small suppliers of large creditworthy buyers because it does not rely on information about the borrower.
- Equity financing is another area for potential growth given that this is particularly important in the early stages of an SME and when debt financing is not an option or the firm has reached its leverage limit.
- Venture capitalists, angel financiers and private equity funds can play a particularly important role where SME stock exchanges are lacking necessary scale, demand and infrastructure.
- Access to finance is also vital for innovation and firm productivity.

  — Studies of the link between access to finance and innovation in developing countries (including MENA

countries) suggest that financing from foreign banks has a much larger impact than financing from local banks, both in promoting innovation such as introducing new product lines and technologies as well as opening a new plant and establishing new foreign joint ventures, and licensing agreements.
— Moreover, firms tend to be more innovative if their borrowing is in a foreign currency.

o In the MENA region, SME lending is constrained by weak financial infrastructure and inefficiencies.

- More than 85% of banks in a recent survey report offering loans to SMEs as well as deposit and cash management accounts, trade finance and payments and transfers.

  — Thus, SME finance is broader than SME lending.

- However, in practice, neither leasing nor factoring is relatively developed among MENA banks.
- Incentives to expand into the SME market are significant and include potential profitability, saturation of the large corporate market, the need to enhance returns and the desire to diversify risks.
- However, in practice, larger banks have not played a significant role in SME financing in MENA.
- Rather banks with a larger branch network and/or that have set up SME units seem to do more SME lending.

o Among the challenges cited by banks in expanding SME lending is the lack of SME transparency and weak financial infrastructure (collateral infrastructure, weak credit information, weak creditor rights).

- In particular, high collateral requirements and difficulties in registration and enforcement of collateral remain obstacles for both borrowers and lenders.
- Less than half of the banks in the region have developed internal scoring models to assess the risk of current and prospective clients and an even smaller share makes use of external credit scoring.

- There is also a weak credit-reporting system and limited reliance on quality of internal credit scores.
- In countries where creditor rights are stronger and more information is provided to creditors, there has been more SME lending overall or more long-term lending to SMEs.
  - ○ In addition, banks cite difficulties with regulatory obstacles (interest rate ceilings), excessive competition in the SME market or lack of demand for loans from SMEs.
  - ○ State-owned banks still play an important role in SME financing with average shares of SME lending roughly similar to private banks.
    - In some cases, state banks take greater risks than private banks in SME lending although they tend to have less developed SME lending technologies and risk management systems.
    - Lower shares of state banks also have dedicated SME units and fewer make use of credit scoring and stress tests.
    - A smaller share of state banks offer payments and transfers or trade finance, relative to private banks and are more focused on conventional SME lending.

- Protection of property rights and a level playing field are important for firm growth and innovation.
  - ○ MENA firm surveys consistently point to uncertainty and lack of a level playing field that favors incumbent firms at the expense of new entrants and competitors as being primary barriers.
    - Firms in Lebanon, for example, cite several modes of unfair competition including special subsidies to privileged firms or protection to informal firms operating in blatant disregard of the law.
  - ○ While on paper, business regulations in the MENA region are generally comparable to more dynamic economies in East Asia, Eastern Europe and others, discretion and favoritism in implementation distorts the business environment.

- Firm survey results in Morocco and Jordan, for example, reveal large variations across firms in wait times for different regulatory services, relative to other emerging economies.
- In particular, the dispersion of wait time for imports to clear customs, to obtain a construction permit or to obtain an operating or import license across firms is among the highest in Jordan across a sample of countries.
- As noted in Sec. II, politically connected firms also have considerable advantages in doing business in MENA countries.

- Firm-level characteristics and organization also matter.
  - Firm ownership and legal organization are important determinants of growth and innovation.
  - State-owned enterprises and family-owned firms are highly prevalent in the MENA region.
    - Empirically, global studies of firms in developing countries including the MENA region suggest that privately-owned firms are in general more innovative than state-owned enterprises.

      — State-owned enterprises are less likely to introduce new products, upgrade existing products, introduce new technology, open new plants, or sign new joint ventures or licensing agreements than privately-owned firms.

    - Moreover, domestic firms are more likely to close existing plants or bring in house previously outsourced activities whereas foreign ownership increases the probability that a firm will sign a new joint venture with a foreign partners and new licensing agreements.
    - Private firms whose controlling shareholder is a financial institution also tend to be less innovative.
    - Firms organized as corporations are more innovative than firms organized as proprietorships, partnerships, or cooperatives.

- With respect to family ownership, the evidence suggests that the identity of the controlling shareholder is particularly important for a firm's propensity to introduce new products, new technology, open new plants, sign joint ventures and licensing agreements.

  — For example, if the controlling shareholder is an individual or a family or the manager of the firm, firms tend to be more innovative than if the largest shareholder is the government.

o Education and human capital play an important role in increasing the likelihood of survival of new firms and improving their post entry growth.

  - In general, the average number of years of previous experience for MENA managers is close to 14 years about twice as high as East Asia.

  - Firm analysis for developing countries including the MENA region suggests that firms run by managers with 3 to 10 years of experience tend to be more innovative than firms run by inexperienced managers. This applies particularly to introducing new products and technology and upgrading existing product lines.

  - However, skill is also vital at the level of the workforce. Firms with a workforce of more than 12 years of education tend to be more innovative.

    — This is particularly critical in high tech sectors where local access to knowledge and founder's human capital are a key driver of post entry tech startups.

  - Other studies focusing on the Maghreb countries in particular suggest that a firm's export status depends in part on factors such as managers' education, presence of quality certification and availability of export finance or overdraft facilities.

  - Empirically, environments in developing countries where there is an absence of learning opportunities tend to be linked with short average survival rates of new ventures.

o   Addressing information gaps is also critical.

   ▪ More innovative firms also tend to have better "connectedness" to global information through exporting and importing intermediate inputs and FDI, use of the internet and cooperative or licensing agreements such as joint ventures, licensing agreements, and business associations.

   ▪ Technology is also an important factor linked with firm success and growth.

   — If the underlying motivation to start a new firm is linked with innovative projects, then better post entry performance is expected.

   ⇒ Young firms in the science-based and specialized suppliers sectors for example tend to have higher chances of survival than firms in other sectors.

   ▫ Being an innovator boosts expected time of survival by 11% compared with no innovators.

   ⇒ But the impact of innovation on performance is tightly linked to sectoral differences and differential patterns of specialization of countries. In many developing countries, the prevalence of traditional sectors tends to make these environments less fertile for innovation driven entrepreneurship.

   ⇒ In the MENA region, the information and communication technology (ICT) sector has experienced particularly high growth and dynamism.

   ▫ Eskadenia, an ICT company founded in Jordan in 2000 by an entrepreneur from Ericcson rapidly became one of the fastest growing software firms in the Middle East. By 2007–2008, it was exporting 80% of its products to countries in the Middle East, Eastern Europe, and North Africa.

References

Ayyagari, M., A. Demirguc-Kunt, and V. Maksimovic (2011) Small vs. Young Firms Across the World: Contribution to Employment, Job Creation, and Growth. Policy Research Working Paper No. WPS 5631. Washington, DC: World Bank.

Beck, T., A. Demirguc-Kunt, and R. Levine (2005) SMEs, Growth and Poverty. NBER Working Paper No. 11224.

Chaffour, J. (2014) *From Political to Economic Awakening in the Arab World: The Path of Economic Integration*. Washington DC: World Bank.

Elbadawi, I. and N. Loayza (2008) Informality, Employment and Economic Development in the Arab World. *Journal of Development and Economic Studies* 10(2): 27–75.

Hallward-Driemeier, M. and F. Thompson (2009) Creative Destruction and Policy Reforms: Changing Productivity Effects of Firm Turnover in Moroccan Manufacturing. World Bank Working Paper 5085, 200.

McMillan, M. and D. Rodrik (2011) Globalization, Structural Change and Productivity Growth. NBER Working Paper No. 17143. Cambridge Massachusetts: National Bureau of Economic Research.

Rijkers, B., H. Arrouri, C. Freund, and A. Nucifora (2014) Which Firms Create The Most Jobs In Developing Countries? Evidence from Tunisia. World Bank Policy Research Working Paper No. 7068.

Rocha, R., S. Farazi, R. Khouri, and D. Pearce (2011) The Status of Bank Lending to SMEs in the Middle East and North Africa Region: The Results of a Joint Survey of the Union of Arab Banks and the World Bank. Policy Research Working Paper No. WPS 5607. Washington DC: World Bank.

Schiffbauer, M., A.Sy, S. Hussain, Sahar, H. Sahnoun, and P. Keefer (2015) *Jobs or Privileges: Unleashing the Employment Potential of the Middle East and North Africa*. Washington, DC: World Bank.

Schneider, F., A. Buehn, and C. Montenegro (2010) Shadow Economies All Over the World. New Estimates for 162 Countries from 1999 to 2007. World Bank Policy Research Working Paper No. 5356.

Sekkat, K. (ed.) (2010) *Market Dynamics and Productivity in Developing Countries*. New York: Springer-Verlag.

Stone, A. and L. Badawy (2011) SME Innovators and Gazelles in MENA: Educate, Train, Certify, Compete! MENA Knowledge and Learning Quick Notes Series No. 43. Washington DC: World Bank.

World Bank (2009) *From Privilege to Competition: Unlocking Private Sector Led Growth in the Middle East and North Africa*. MENA Development Report. Washington DC: World Bank.

Chapter 8

Poverty and Social Welfare in the MENA Region

Relative to other developing regions, Middle East and North Africa (MENA) countries have low levels of poverty and a relatively equitable income distribution. Moreover, from a historical perspective, governments in the region have tended to spend more on the unemployed, the disabled, and the poor, relative to levels in industrialized countries at historically similar levels of per capita income.

Nevertheless, MENA households are highly vulnerable to changes in economic conditions and closely clustered around the poverty line. An estimated 17% of Egyptians, 15% of Yemenis, and 10% of Moroccans have consumption levels of not more than 50 cents per day, above US$2 per day. The region is also characterized by pockets of chronic and high poverty incidence and marginalized groups with limited access to social services and economic opportunities.

This chapter explores underlying drivers of poverty and inequality in the MENA region and potential measures to improve social welfare. Section I discusses the overall nature of poverty and inequality in the region, while Section II reviews trends in poverty incidence and inequality over time. Section III discusses social welfare programs and policy measures to enhance social welfare.

I. Inequality and Poverty in the MENA Region[1]

- In general, inequality across developing countries, as measured by the variability of Gini coefficients across countries is large compared with changes in Gini coefficients within countries over time.

  o This suggests that inequality is linked with factors which differ substantially across countries but tend to be relatively stable within countries over time.

- History, politics, market forces, factor endowments, and government policy, all affect how income is divided.

  o Land reform — in South Korea, land redistribution led to a relatively equal distribution of rural income.
  o Colonial economy and natural resources — large farms and high dependence on minerals are generally linked with greater inequality.
  o Large public sectors, employment and legislated wages lowered inequality in Eastern Europe and Former Soviet Union.
  o Access to high quality education, Social Safety Nets (SSNs), taxes, and government spending, all matter for inequality.

- Latin America and the Caribbean (LAC), and Sub-Saharan Africa (SSA) tend to have the highest Gini coefficients, followed by East Asia and the Pacific, and MENA which have more equal income distributions.

  o In 2010, Gini coefficients for a sample of MENA countries averaged 36, relative to 44 in SSA, 43 in Latin America, and 40 on average for developing countries.
  o However, other databases show higher income inequality or Gini coefficients for MENA countries, estimated at 47.

- Looking beyond Gini coefficients at decile shares of household consumption, on average, the poorest 10% of the population in

---

[1] This discussion is based on Silva *et al.* (2013), Iqbal (2006), World Bank (2011), Alvaredo & Gasparini (2013), Marotta *et al.* (2011), Thirwall (2006).

a country accrues less than 3% of total consumption while the top 10% accounts for 32%.

- o In a typical developing country, aggregate consumption of the poorest 60% of the population is smaller than the consumption of the top 10%.

- Moreover, while countries in the world appear significantly different in the consumption share of the poor and the rich, they are more similar in shares of the middle strata, particularly the upper-middle strata.

- o Aggregate consumption shares of deciles five to nine, for example, are around 50% on average and very stable across countries.
- o Some analysts have called this the homogenous middle.
- o Moreover, variability is actually smaller across countries in the upper-middle deciles with the proportion of total consumption accruing to this group quite similar in all geographic regions of the world and ranging from 36% in SSA to 37% in Europe and Central Asia (ECA).
- o Thus, the main difference across regions appears to lie in the share of the bottom 60% compared to the upper 10%.

- What about the trends in inequality?

- o On average, levels of national income inequality across developing countries increased during the 1980s and 1990s, and declined in the 2000s.

  - Ginis were basically unchanged between 1981 and 1987 and increased to 40.5 in 1999, falling after 2002 to 39.4 in 2010.
  - Most of the increase during the 1980s was linked with rising inequality in ECA after the fall of Communism, whereas the decline in the 2000s was widespread, although it was more intense in regions such as LAC.
  - Shares of the "middle" remained relatively stable over the last two decades.

- Moreover, gaps in inequality among regions are smaller now than they were two decades ago.

• In the MENA region, there is limited data. Most studies are based on a handful of countries — in this case, Egypt, Iran, Jordan, Morocco, and Tunisia.

  o Four periods can be discerned.

    ▪ The period until 1985 was characterized by rapid economic growth and a large reduction in income inequality between the mid-1970s and the early 1990s.
    ▪ The second period of the late 1980s and most of the 1990s is characterized by low economic growth and limited gains in real per capita income with a stable income distribution.
    ▪ In the 2000s, however, there has been a downward trend in inequality although at a slow pace.

    — Mean Ginis fell from 38.7 in 2002 to 36.8 in 2010.

  o Thus, some analysts point out that somewhat surprisingly, MENA is a region of moderate inequality in the developing world.

    ▪ As one author puts it, "In many MENA countries, from the Maghreb to the Arabian Peninsula, power is wielded by rather narrow groups .... Seen from this perspective, the most puzzling thing about inequality in the Middle East is how low it is" (Robinson, 2009).

  o Studies based on a regional perspective however find that income inequality is extremely large at the level of the Middle East taken as a whole, simply because regional inequality in per capita Gross National Product (GNP) is so large.

    ▪ This study estimates that the top 10% of the income share could be well over 60% and the top 1% share might exceed 25% versus 20% in the US, 9% in Western Europe, and 18% in South Africa.

- Most of the world's poor live in middle-income countries. The MENA region however has generally low levels of poverty relative to other middle-income regions.
  - In 2010, about 41% of the population lived with less than US$2 per day; in the MENA region, it is about 13% (2010).
  - Across developing regions, countries in ECA tend to have the lowest poverty incidence, followed by MENA and LAC.
- However, diversity within the region remains high.
  - Poverty headcount ratios at US$2 per day range from less than 2% in the West Bank and Gaza, and Jordan to over 40% in Yemen and Iraq.
- Absolute poverty is not very prevalent although chronic poverty is concentrated in specific groups.
- Overall, the number of poor in the MENA region is estimated to be about 40–50 million people (2005–2010).
- Large changes in the number of poor tend to occur at different poverty lines suggesting high vulnerability to poverty incidence.
  - Poverty incidence for the MENA region as a whole increases to approximately 22% for a US$2.50 per day poverty line (2011).
    - At the US$4.00 poverty line, the poverty rate increases to 50% (2011).
  - This suggests a degree of vulnerability to poverty incidence and a large number of near-poor.
    - An estimated 17% of Egyptians, 15% of Yemenis, and 10% of Moroccans have consumption levels of no more than 50 cents per day, above US$2 per day.
  - Vulnerability — the concept of vulnerability captures the likelihood that people will fall into poverty owing to shocks to the economic system or personal mishaps.

- It is a reflection of economic insecurity.
- Moreover, vulnerable households must rely on their own income, savings and assets, as well as informal safety nets (private support from family and neighbors) in the event of shocks.

o National poverty lines and household survey data in Egypt, Iraq, Syria, and Yemen confirm that a high share of the population hovers just above the poverty line.

- Thus, in the MENA region, vulnerable households constitute a large share of the population.
- As noted above, they are also vulnerable to even smaller income losses.

— An estimated 15% of households in Iraq and Morocco, for example, suffered at least one major shock during the previous 12 months. Moreover, formal safety nets do not generally reach these households.
— Only 1% of households experiencing a major shock in Iraq and Morocco reported receiving help from formal safety nets.

o Much of this vulnerability is linked with low levels of disposable income and high shares of total expenditures on essentials that cannot be easily scaled down in the event of shocks.

- In Jordan, rising costs of food and basic goods caused an increase in poverty incidence among vulnerable groups.

— Wages did not rise and vulnerable households which allocated 43.5% of household expenditures to food suffered.
— Asset ownership represented only 0.9% of average household income suggesting limited scope for asset sales to deal with higher expenditures.

- In Egypt, households in the three poorest quintiles allocated 88% of household consumption to basic goods — 62% of household income was generated by salaries and

33% by transfers. Between 2005 and 2008, 55% of Egyptians experienced at least one episode of poverty or near poverty.

- Is poverty a spatial phenomenon?
  - In other words, are the poor concentrated in certain locations and geographic areas? Yes, and household characteristics also play a role, in particular fertility and education rates.
  - In Syria, for example, average per capita household consumption in 2004 in the richest province, Damascus, was 90% higher than in the poorest province, El Quneitra.
    - More generally, poverty rates tend to be highest in semi-arid, desert, and mountainous areas where population density is lowest, but there are also large numbers of absolute poor living in urban areas.
  - In Libya, the highest poverty rates can be found in Al Kufrah, Ghat, and Mizdah.
    - Al Kurfah is a desert in the Southeast, bordering Egypt and Sudan on the East and Chad on the South. The capital, Al Jawf, receives less than 3 mm of rain per year.
    - Ghat is also a desert province in the far Southwest bordering Algeria; Mizdah is a hilly area further in the North.
    - All three provinces have a combined population of 81,000 according to the 1995 census of which 25,000 were living below the poverty line.
    - On the other hand, Benghazi, a coastal province had an estimated 50,000 people living in poverty despite a much lower poverty rate.
  - Similarly in Iraq, poverty rates in 2009 were about 10% in Kirkuk and 13% in Baghdad while Babel, Muthanna, and Sala'alddin governorates had poverty rates above 40%.
    - However, in terms of absolute numbers, the poor were concentrated in big cities — 13% living in Baghdad and another 11% in Basra.

- Overall, there were a third more poor people living in Iraq's four richest governorates than in the four poorest governorates.

  o Household characteristics also play a role.

    - In Egypt, for example, Upper Egypt has only 40% of the population of Egypt but accounts for 60% of its poverty and 80% of severe poverty.

      — However, demographic factors (large families) explain about 62% of the consumption gap between Upper and Lower Egypt.
      — Upper Egypt has high dependency ratios or the ratio of dependents to people of working age.

    - In Jordan, average rural per capita consumption is about 24% less than urban levels in Jordan, but if demographic differences are removed, this shrinks to 12% and controlling for educational disparities, this gap shrinks to 3%.
    - Morocco, on the other hand, has a significant — urban–rural gap which remains high even accounting for household characteristics.
    - Per capita household consumption in rural areas is roughly 54% of levels in urban areas and the gap remains as high as 41% if demographic factors are controlled for.
    - Accounting for education does not shrink the gap much — it remains high at 32%.

- What about spatial gaps in inequality?

  o In Jordan, there is little difference between rural and urban measures while in Egypt and Morocco, rural–urban divides explain 16–29% of inequality.

    - This is roughly in line with global norms.

- What about interprovincial inequality — or differences within provinces, governorates, and others?

  o Interprovincial inequality appears to be a relatively small component of overall inequality for Syria, Jordan, and Yemen.

o   However, in Egypt and Lebanon, it accounts for more than a fifth of total inequality.
o   In Morocco, interprovincial disparities in ownership of assets such as housing, livestock, land, and consumer durables account for nearly 30% of overall economic inequality while measures based on consumption such as household expenditure suggest that interprovincial inequality is a very small part of overall inequality.

- Who are the poor? Globally, the typical extremely poor family tends to be rather large, at least by the standards of today's rich countries. Some characteristics of poor households in developing countries include the following:

o   Family size ranges from 6 to 12 with many children.
o   Food typically represents 56% to 78% of expenditures among rural households and 56% to 74% in urban areas.
o   Apart from land, extremely poor households in rural areas tend to own very little by way of durable goods, including productive assets.
o   Temporary migration to work.
o   Low educational attainment.
o   Weak health and nutrition — low calorie intake, frequent illnesses.
o   Many of the extremely poor households operate their own businesses, but do so with almost no productive assets.
o   Limited ability to insure against risks.
o   Multiple jobs, little specialization, lack of scale.
o   Average landholding for those who own land is usually quite small and renting land is infrequent.

- More generally, important demographic factors affecting household consumption and poverty include

o   Size of the household — the more household members, the lower the consumption per capita for a given level of earnings.
o   Number of people of working age in the household.
o   Number of females in the household because there are cultural limitations on women's earning opportunities.

o Gender of the head of the household because female and male households have different opportunities to access markets and services on behalf of household members.
o Age of the head of the household — since earning power typically peaks in midlife and falls as old age approaches.
o What about education? More educated households tend to do better than households with less education, wherever they are located.

   ▪ In general, leading areas have a higher share of well-educated people so part of the differences between leading and lagging areas tends to be education.
   ▪ This can be affected by both supply and demand factors. Education services may be better supplied in leading areas and parents may be better off and better able to afford better education.

- Who are the poor in MENA?
   o In general, the poor are predominately young, rural, uneducated, and employed in the private informal economy.
   o For the region as a whole, childhood poverty is high, both in low and middle income countries and relative to comparators.

   ▪ In Jordan, for example, more than 20% of all children are poor, along with 36% in Yemen and nearly 30% in Egypt and Iraq.
   ▪ Children in the poorest quintiles are much less likely to have access to services.

      — In Jordan, a 10 year old girl in the poorest quintile is 40% less likely to drink treated water and 50% less likely to have a bed than a girl in the richest quintile.

   ▪ Childhood malnutrition is strikingly high, particularly in Egypt, Iraq, Kuwait, Libya, Morocco, Syria, and Yemen and given per capita income levels.

      — Stunting (low height for age) rates of children under five in Yemen are as high as 60%.

— Factors contributing to this include levels of economic development as well as food intake and poor nutrition practices.

- Malnutrition affects lifelong prospects with irreversible impacts:

    — It increases risks of morbidity and mortality, impairs cognitive development and reduces productivity later in life.

o Access to health services is also skewed across income groups including from early childhood which has lifelong consequences.

- Basic coverage rates for basic health outcomes are highest for the richest quintiles and lowest for the poorest.
- Vaccination rates differ significantly by wealth with children in the poorest quintiles much less likely to have all of their vaccinations.
- Poorer households also report lack of access to funds to cover healthcare costs as a problem two to four times more often than wealthier households.

    — An estimated 55% of the poor claim that cost constrains access to healthcare in Morocco and 50% report distance to health facilities as a problem.

- Under conditions of perfect equality of opportunity, circumstances such as a child's location or gender should have no impact on his or her basic human development outcomes so that distribution of outcomes would be the same for any circumstance group.

o Average heads of poor households in the MENA region are uneducated, between the ages of 45 and 50 and provide for a family of five or more members.

- This is in line with global poverty profiles.

o Poor children also suffer from low access to education.

- In general, the MENA region has low access to preschool with only 22% of young children attending preschool, relative to 47% in South Asia and 69% in LAC.

  — In Iraq and Syria, enrollment in pre primary education is less than 10%.

- Poor children also have lower completion rates for primary education, higher dropout rates and more limited access to higher education than non-poor children.

  — In Egypt, primary non-completion is 5.7% for children from poor households and 0.5% for children from non-poor households.
  — Access to higher education is limited even for poor youth who complete secondary schooling.

    ⇒ In Egypt, the poorest quintile of the population represents only 4% of higher education students — in Jordan, there are three times as many students from the richest quintile as those from the poorest quintile.

- Poverty in MENA is also linked with weak asset ownership and quality.

  o In rural areas, poverty incidence is higher among small landowners.
  o In rural Tunisia, 43% of farm families own less than 5 ha and control 6% of arable land.

- Unlike other developing regions, poverty is not necessarily concentrated among female-headed households.

  o However, labor force participation is limited for women, given the cultural barriers, weak support systems, and wage distribution.

    - Moreover, a woman cannot apply for a family allowance unless she can prove that her husband is deceased or disabled or that she is the primary breadwinner.

o Female-headed households also represent a relatively small portion of total households, ranging from 5% in Kuwait to 17% in Morocco.
o Female-headed households rely more heavily on transfers from friends and family relative to male-headed households.

  ▪ However, this proportion appears to be growing as a result of rising rates of divorce and increasing life expectancy.

• The MENA's poor have limited mobility, low pay, and low quality jobs.

o The poor are mostly low-skilled and are likely to have precarious employment due to lack of means to move into better jobs.
o Informal workers are estimated to earn between 10% and 20% lower salaries than formal workers with similar skills.

  ▪ In Egypt and Tunisia, more than half of the workers do not have a contract.

o Adult males in poor families tend to be employed more in the informal sector and in Egypt and Morocco have less access to public sector employment.

  ▪ Whereas public sector employment offers social protection and the formal private sector offers high wages, sectors where the poor tend to work are neither protected nor high paying.

o Among youth, poverty strongly increases the chances to be out of school and out of work.

  ▪ In Egypt, Jordan, and Morocco, the likelihood of poor young men to be in this state is twice as high as that of young men in higher income families.
  ▪ In rural Morocco, more than 40% of young men in the bottom two quintiles were out of school and out of work in 2010 compared with only 20% of those in the top two quintiles. Lack of experience and post basic education

create joblessness at a young age and affect future earnings potential.

- Low mobility. The poor also show higher persistence in low quality jobs and have a higher likelihood of falling out of good quality jobs.

  — Unlike other developing regions, informality is also not a temporary phenomenon.

  — Studies for Egypt show that the persistence of various labor market outcomes varies a lot with the individual's household consumption levels.

  — Among youth with low paying informal jobs in the bottom two household quintiles in 2008, 73% were in the same status a year later compared with only 65% among the same cohort from the top two household wealth quintiles.

  — Wealthier workers are less likely to be in low quality jobs and better able to move out of them.

  — In addition, a more recent study of labor market opportunities in Egypt, suggests that the chances of finding quality employment are highly linked with parents' educational levels and occupation, suggesting low levels of economic and social mobility.

  — Many poor are also lacking jobs altogether — in Jordan and Morocco, households in lower income quintiles are those most likely to have no members employed with 25% and 36% of households respectively with no members employed.

- As noted earlier, the poor in MENA have low vulnerability to shocks.

  o High food prices can create significant losses of assets or income, given high shares of expenditures on basic necessities.

    - 58% of households in Iraq suffering major shocks reported reducing the quantity and quality of food consumed.

o In other cases, loss of an asset or livestock due to violence or theft is the most common source of vulnerability.

- As many as 15% of households in Iraq, Morocco, and Egypt reported suffering at least one major shock in the previous 12 months.
- In Yemen, this included death of household member, serious injury or illness, and loss of assets due to violence and theft together with job losses.
- In Iraq, conflict related mortality and morbidities have been associated with increased asset sales by households, higher school dropout rates and worse health outcomes for children.

o Catastrophic health care costs are a particular problem.
o Limited access to formal safety nets.

II. Trends in Poverty

- Over the last three decades, there has been a significant decline in absolute poverty. This accelerated during the 2000s — in only 8 out of 121 countries did poverty increase between 1999 and 2010 — the majority in SSA.

  o For the MENA region on average, poverty declined by 43% from the 1990s to the 2000s.

- Analysts typically decompose changes in poverty into growth and redistribution effects, in order to characterize poverty trends.

  o Growth effects refer to the poverty change between two years that would have occurred if the mean income had changed as it did, but the shape of the distribution had remained fixed.

  o Alternatively, the redistribution effect captures the poverty change between two years that would have occurred if the shape of the distribution had changed in the way that it did but the mean had remained fixed.

o Such decompositions, while useful, do not however give information on the fundamental factors driving poverty changes and on the policies recommended to reduce poverty effectively.

- For most developing countries, including the MENA region, changes in growth-inequality and poverty were very different in the 2000s relative to previous years.

  o In general, declines in the poverty headcount ratio in the 1990s were more directly linked with a poverty decreasing growth effect that outweighed a poverty increasing redistribution effect.

    ▪ Mean consumption grew by about US$0.2 per year whereas the Gini increased by about 0.3 points per year, implying a modest decline in poverty.

  o During the 2000s, both effects worked in the same direction to reduce poverty.

    ▪ Mean consumption grew by more than 3% per year while inequality declined (by around 0.1 Gini points per year) which worked together to yield large reductions in poverty.

    ▪ For most countries, the growth effect was particularly large, accounting for about 90% of the decline in the headcount poverty ratio.

    ▪ While changes in distribution were important they were not the primary drivers.

- Historically, most of the decline in poverty in MENA occurred during the 1960s and 1970s:

  o With average rates of per capita growth of over 4.5% between 1975 and 1984 together with a relatively equitable income distribution, poverty decreased substantially.

    ▪ In Tunisia, for example, an estimated 51% of the population was living in poverty in 1965 relative to 16% in 1985.

  o In Egypt, poverty rates fell from 82% to 53% between 1975 and 1985.

o Other studies estimate a regional decline from 57% in the late 1970s to 22% in the early 1990s.

- Poverty reduction however largely stalled during the 1980s and 1990s, particularly over the 1990s.

  o This period was characterized by slow growth and declining remittances and aid flows, together with a low payoff from reforms.

  o On average, real per capita income increased by less than 1.5% per year with the proportion of poor roughly unchanged at 22% for more than a decade.

  o Average poverty incidence fluctuated between 23% and 28% for much of the 1980s and 1990s.

    - Poverty reduction during the 1990s largely stagnated with a decline from 24% in 1990 to 23.5% in 1999.

  o By 2001, approximately 52 million people were poor, an increase in absolute numbers of approximately 11.5 million people compared with the situation in 1987.

  o In MENA, during the 1990s, the redistribution effect dominated the growth effect whereas after 1999, growth effects were significantly more important for poverty reduction.

  o Relative to LAC and ECA however, redistribution effects were much larger in terms of lowering poverty incidence.

- During the 2000s, poverty declined by 43% from 22% in 1999 to about 12% in 2010.

  o The poverty rate in MENA declined over the 1990–2005 period, although at a slower rate than in Latin American countries and Central and Eastern ECA.

  o While the number of people living on less than US$2 per day increased by 7 million in the 1990s alone, this was reduced by 20 million in the 2000s from 60 to 40 million people.

  o Moreover, while in the 1990s poverty declined in only a third of MENA countries, in the 2000s it declined in all economies, with the exception of Yemen.

- The growth elasticity of poverty reduction is usually estimated by regressing the annualized proportional change in poverty indicators against the annualized growth rate of mean income (per capita income or consumption or per capita GDP or aggregate private consumption).

  o Data for a large group of developing countries including the MENA region suggest average rates of −3.1 over the 1981–1994 period for US$1 and a smaller elasticity for higher US$2 per day poverty lines (about −2).

  o During the 2000s, however, the absolute value of the elasticities has increased suggesting that growth was better translated to the poor.

    ▪ From 2005 to 2008, for example, the welfare of the average poor person in Egypt increased by almost 10% per year and was sufficient to move a poor household out of poverty.

III. Social Welfare in the MENA Region — What do we Know?

  o The average MENA country spends about 6% of Gross Domestic Product (GDP) on non-targeted food and energy subsidies.

  o Energy subsidies are on average three-fourths of total subsidy spending.

    ▪ But there is high diversity within the region — in Yemen, energy subsidies account for nearly 14% of GDP relative to food subsidies (0.1% of GDP) whereas in Iraq and Lebanon, food subsidy expenditure outweigh fuel subsidies.

    ▪ In Iraq, the Public Distribution System food ration cards reach nearly all Iraqis and spending is about 6% of GDP.

  o In 2008, spending on fuel subsidies in Egypt was equal to all health and education expenditures combined, while in Syria and Yemen, fuel subsidies were more than 1.5 times combined health and education expenditures.

- o Subsidies are large compared with targeted social assistance.

  - For every US$1 received by the poor in non-subsidy form in Jordan, Iraq, Yemen, and Egypt, around US$24, US$96, US$158, and US$194 are spent on subsidies or ration cards.

- Why subsidies and ration cards?

  - o Subsidies and ration cards aim at achieving a number of objectives including:

    - Expanding access to subsidized goods.
    - To promote development of certain sectors (industry for fuel subsidies and agriculture for food subsidies).
    - To offset temporary commodity price changes.
    - To avoid inflationary pressures.
    - To maintain popular support.

- MENA countries are not unique in providing subsidies to income groups but efficiency is low.

  - o Food subsidies and ration cards in Iraq and Morocco cover almost everyone in the country.

    - In Egypt, food ration cards which require registration miss about 20% of the bottom quintile.

- The richest 20% of the population captures 40–60% of all fuel subsidy benefits because the rich consume more energy products.

  - o In Iran, for example, leakage rates for energy subsidies, that is the share of subsidy accruing to the non-poor is estimated at 94% in urban areas and 89% in rural areas.
  - o More generally, the poorest quintile in Egypt, Jordan, and Lebanon received only 1% to 8% of total gasoline subsidies, while the richest quintile received subsidies of 38–86% of the total (2004–2010).

- There is also a high potential for fraud and corruption with subsidies and ration cards.

  - o Egypt could save about 73% of the cost of food subsidies if it eliminated leakages.

- In Iraq, the Public Distribution system food ration subsidy was estimated to cost US$6.30 to transfer US$1 worth of food while in Egypt it costs US$5.40 to transfer US$1 worth of food to the poor.

- Current efforts underway in some countries to reform untargeted food and energy subsidies include the following:

  - In Morocco, the government increased the price of energy products at different rates, with fuel oil increasing by 27%, gasoline by 20%, and diesel by 14% in June 2012. Subsequently, a partial indexation mechanism for select petroleum products was introduced in September 2013 with the result that diesel prices increased by 8.5%, gasoline by 4.8%, and fuel by 14.2%. By January 2014, the government eliminated subsidies on gasoline and industrial fuel and reduced the per-unit subsidy on diesel.
  - In Jordan, universal subsidies on bread, flour, rice, sugar, and milk were progressively phased out first by increased rationing based on income criteria and introducing self-targeting through the allocation of ration coupons. By the mid-1990s, subsidies on bread and flour were eliminated and replaced with targeted, means-tested cash transfers and later by targeted cash assistance through the National Aid Fund.
  - Jordan also reformed its energy subsidies beginning in 2012 by raising electricity tariffs for selected sectors (banks, telecommunications, hotels, and mining) and large domestic corporations and households. Later that year, it eliminated fuel subsidies and in January 2013 introduced a monthly fuel price adjustment mechanism. In 2013 and 2014 electricity tariffs were increased by 7–15% for select consumers. At the same time, the government introduced cash transfers to families with incomes below a certain income threshold (about 70% of the population) to be made if oil prices are above US$100.

- Social welfare programs are small, highly fragmented, and cover less than 30% of the bottom quintile.

o Most of these are cash transfer programs.

  ▪ In Egypt, the Monthly Pension Program (Sadat Pension) helps families without able bodied males.
  ▪ In Lebanon, most transfers support fee waivers for education and hospitals.
  ▪ In Yemen, half of the expenditures are on workfare.
  ▪ In Morocco, non-cash programs such as community infrastructure projects predominate.
  ▪ In Jordan, training and micro-credit programs take up a large share of the social welfare program budget.

o Coverage rates tend to be low — more than 70% in the poorest quintile receive no income support transfers.

  ▪ These are below what is expected in terms of per capita income.
  ▪ Only 16% of people in the bottom quintile receive social transfers, relative to 50% in ECA and LAC.

    — Coverage of the bottom quintile is less than half of the world average.

  ▪ In Egypt, the Monthly Social Pension program covers only 8% of the poorest quintile; in Jordan, the National Assistance Fund (NAF) covers only about 16.5% of the poorest quintile. Iraq's coverage is less than 2% of the poorest quintile.
  ▪ Exception is the West Bank and Gaza.

• Targeting efficiency is low. Targeting is categorical and geographic, which tends to work well in environments where poverty is concentrated but not where it is multifaceted and spatially dispersed.

  o Targeting is mostly categorical (i.e., well-identified groups — widows, elderly (Bahrain, Egypt, Iraq, Kuwait, Syria) and geographic (Morocco, Yemen).
  o Many countries such as Bahrain, Egypt, Iraq, Kuwait, Saudi Arabia, and Syria rely exclusively on categorical targeting (i.e., widows, orphans).

o   In Morocco and Yemen, targeting is heavily linked with geographic targeting.
o   Use of means testing is much less common with the exception of Jordan and Tunisia which use income thresholds as edibility cutoffs.

   ▪ However, Proxy Means Testing is an emerging trend in programs in Lebanon, Morocco, West Bank, Gaza, and Yemen. Some programs are self-targeted.

o   About one quarter of social welfare program beneficiaries come from the poorest quintile, whereas 15% of beneficiaries come from the richest quintile except in Egypt, Jordan, West Bank, and Gaza.

   ▪ In Morocco, the share of the poorest is the same as that of the richest, implying hardly any targeting.
   ▪ In Iraq, the distribution of beneficiaries is skewed towards the rich with the top quintile making up 30% of beneficiaries.
   ▪ In all other regions, the bottom quintiles constitute about 30% or more of beneficiaries.

      — Iraq and Morocco stand out in terms of targeting relative to per capita income.

   ▪ In well-designed programs, the bottom quintile receives the most transfers with the share of transfers falling as wealth increases.

      — In Jordan's NAF, for example, the richest two quintiles receive less than 20% of all NAF transfers.

   ▪ The average program distributes only 23% of benefits to the lowest quintile relative to nearly 60% in comparators.

o   The transfer size of social welfare programs is small.
o   The generosity of programs reaching bottom quintiles is low, constituting less than 15% of welfare of the bottom quintile.

- Jordan, West Bank, and Gaza have the greatest benefits for the poor.
- In Egypt, transfers are more generous for the richest quintile relative to the poorest.
  o The impact of transfers on poverty and inequality is weak.
    - With the exception of the West Bank and Gaza and Jordan, transfers have little effect on poverty rates.
    - In Egypt, Iraq, and Yemen, for example, it is estimated that these programs reduce poverty rates by at most 4%.
      — This is much worse than the world average or in ECA and LAC.
    - Empirical evidence for social transfers in Jordan, the West Bank and Gaza suggests that they do however reduce the poverty gap by 23% and 42%, respectively.
      — In Egypt and Iraq, transfers reduce the poverty gap by about 7%, whereas in Yemen it is 4%.
  o What about inequality?
    - In the West Bank and Gaza, transfers appear to have some impact on reducing the Gini coefficient by more than 7% whereas most other programs have little impact.
    - In Egypt, Iraq, and Yemen there is no apparent impact, the Gini coefficient falls by less than 1%.

- Privately funded and informal systems play a significant role in some countries.
  o Such transfers tend to be represented by in-kind gifts, income support to family members, and supplier credit.
  o MENA countries have strong family structures and social networks in which households rely on members or relatives to offset the effects of crises and loss of income.
    - In Jordan, for example, it is estimated that 40% of those aged 60 or older live with their children.

- Household surveys in the West Bank and Gaza, for example, suggest that nearly one-half of households give assistance to family and relatives — mostly in the form of gifts for religious and social occasions.

  ○ About 10% give regular, informal support to other individuals or families within their kinship group and only 4% give regular assistance to individuals of families outside their kinship group.

- In rural communities in Yemen, family support is enhanced with informal lines of supplier credit.

  ○ A 1998 study of rural households living on less than US$200 per month indicated that more than half of the survey sample was in debt to relatives or neighbors (47% total) and local retailers and traders (42%).

  ○ Levels of debt ranged from four times monthly income or US$100 (60% total) to US$200 (15% of total), and up to US$500 (9%).

  ○ Unpaid or partially paid debt was largely a running line of credit, with households paying off what they could when they were able.

- Rendering part of the economic returns on assets to the poor in the form of *zakat* or a wealth tax is a central pillar of Islam.

  ○ In some countries, *zakat* funds are collected and administered by the state; in others collection and distribution is private and voluntary.

  ○ In many cases, collection and expenditure of *zakat* revenues is somewhat unpredictable; at times funds remain unspent while distribution is at times, sporadic.

    ■ In Yemen, for example, inflow of *zakat* funds is concentrated during Ramadan and Eid and provides a major source of social protection but tends to ebb and flow through the remainder of the year.

    ■ Nevertheless, a study of 795 households suggests that *zakat* can be an important source of income (particularly during Ramadan) and relatively well targeted to the chronic poor in Yemen.

— 30% of all households in Yemen give *zakat* — generally the amount is less than 2.5% of annual income.
— Generally, receivers were known by givers — the majority of donors lived near givers.

⇒ 82% of givers donated to those in the Household (HH) or near HH; 60% gave to the same group for more than 3 years.

IV. Raising Social Welfare in the MENA Region

- There is a need for a multifaceted approach to improving social welfare systems in the MENA region.
- First, well-designed social welfare programs can promote inclusion and productivity (by focusing on human development related outcomes) but they are not a substitute for growth.

  o Higher economic growth is needed first and foremost to sustain recent gains in poverty reduction and enhance social welfare.

- Second, there is a need to reform untargeted food and fuel subsidies.

  o A number of countries in the region such as Morocco and Jordan have made progress in this regard but more can be done. Success measures include:

    ▪ Raising fuel prices until they reach international parity (fuel oil and kerosene);
    ▪ Introducing increases in the minimum wage or cash transfer to help mitigate the impact on poorer households. In Jordan, a one-time bonus was also extended to low income government employees together with cash transfers to low income households.

- Third, existing social welfare programs need to be consolidated, better targeted to the poor and better resourced, so as to transfer sufficient benefits to reduce poverty incidence.
- This requires a number of actions including:
  - Identifying different risks faced by the poor and ensuring that programs are available to help families address these risks.
    - Many of the region's social welfare programs leave poor and vulnerable groups either uncovered or partially covered.
    - Gaps in coverage and benefit size are an issue, as well as missing programs such as nutrition programs, education or programs to promote behavioral change to improve child nutrition or insurance that does not adequately finance hospital care or medicines.
  - Introducing Proxy Means Targeting as an efficient way to ensure that the poor are adequately targeted through social welfare assistance.
    - Categorical targeting on the other hand, focused on widows etc., irrespective of their poverty levels can result in leakages to the non-needy, as well as provide undercoverage of the poor who do not fit in these categories.
      - It also limits the ability of programs to scale up when governments try to reach beneficiaries who do not fit in any of the predefined categories.
      - It may also negatively associate a program with charity and stigmatize recipients.
  - Proxy Means Testing generates a score for each household based on observable characteristics such as education, household size, location, quality of dwelling, and ownership of durable goods. Information provided by applicants is usually verified by a home visit from a program official or by having the applicant give written verification of the

information. Eligibility is determined by comparing the household's score against a predetermined cutoff. This method tends to be fairly accurate in identifying the poor, can be quickly implemented and works for national scale programs. It is also a good alternative to means testing, where there are many informal workers or where data is less available.

o Other possibilities are community-based targeting and self-targeting.

   ▪ With community-based targeting, non-recipients decide who should benefit.

   ▪ With self-targeting, recipients receive lower wages at the bottom of unskilled labor scale or programs subsidize lower quality items.

o Based on the nature and extent of risks, a small number of programs can be expanded or effectively consolidated.

   ▪ Examples include Early Childhood Development programs to address malnutrition and promote early child stimulation and development, Conditional Cash Transfers (CCTs) which link cash assistance to undertake basic health care and enrollment in schools, public on-the-job training for youth with NGOs and private sector participation, as well as community driven development funds.

   ▪ This could also include scaling up of successful programs. Morocco's Tayssir program and the West Bank and Gaza Cash Transfer Programs are good examples of successful programs which can be scaled up.

o Develop a strategy for implementation of the reform and a national database for targeting.

   ▪ In the MENA region, public consultation exercises suggest that there is ample support for better targeting of social assistance programs to the poor.

- — However, there is little support for making such transfers conditional on behavioral actions by the recipient households such as school attendance or health clinic visits.

- A single registry system can effectively serve as the main instrument for coordination and convergence of social welfare programs and allows administrators to quickly assess needs, and target and monitor poor and vulnerable households.

References

Alvaredo, F. and L. Gasparini (2013) Recent Trends in Inequality and Poverty in Developing Countries. Centro de Estudios Distributivos, Laborales y Sociales Working Paper No. 151.

Iqbal, F. (2006) *Sustaining Gains in Poverty Reduction and Human Development in the Middle East and North Africa.* Washington DC: World Bank.

Marotta, D. R. Yemtsov, H. El-Laithy, H. Abou-Ali, and S. Al-Shawarby (2011) Was Growth in Egypt Between 2005 and 2008 Pro-Poor? World Bank Policy Research Working Paper Series, No. 5589. World Bank.

Robinson, J. (2009) The Political Economy of Inequality. Economic Research Forum Working Paper No. 493.

Silva, J., V. Levin, and M. Morgandi (2013) *Inclusion and Resilience. The Way Forward For Social Safety Nets in the Middle East and North Africa.* MENA Development Report. Washington DC: International Bank for Reconstruction and Development.

World Bank (2011) *Poor Places: Thriving People.* MENA Development Report. Washington DC: International Bank for Reconstruction and Development.

Index

Printed in the United States
By Bookmasters